JOYFUL SENIORS

NEW INSIGHTS TO INCREASE HAPPINESS

S.V. RAMAN

ISBN 979-8-88530-358-3

Contents

About the Author

S.V.Raman, 71 years, is an engineering consultant. Earlier, he retired as Senior Project Manager from a Multi National Company. During his career spanning more than four decades, he had worked and travelled across all regions of India, besides a stint of three years in Netherlands.

His earlier book titled "Arranged Marriage – Guide to finalise compatible alliance", published in 2017 received accolades from luminaries from diverse fields and helped many to find their life partners.

He has also published numerous articles on diverse subjects and genre, in English National Daily, Tamil literary magazine and other forms of print and digital media.

About: "Joyful Seniors – New Insights To Increase Happiness"

If you are a senior citizen or an adult with elderly parent(s), then this book is destined to increase your happiness as it is based on extensive research comprising studies, interactions, introspection and meditation spread over five years.

The outcome is authentic with latest insights on every relevant topic, including those which are usually shied away from.

True to the subject, the reading itself would bring you delight thanks to simple language combined with wit and wisdom.

Not convinced?

Read the reviews from eminent persons from diverse fields.

Reviews

. . . .

Joyful Seniors – New Insights To Increase Happiness

Dr. Ananth, S. Fellow of Royal Australian College of General Physician.

Congratulations Mr. Raman for the fantastic work. This book is comprehensive and a MUST READ for all the senior citizens. Among the many features that I enjoyed include: very easy to read; good sketches; introduction and summary given in every chapter etc. I am sure this book will be a big success.

Mr. Banerjee Robin. Managing Director, Caprihans India Ltd.

Another amazing and enjoyable book by Mr. Raman, which is superbly structured containing well outlined ideas. Though intended for seniors, it would be liked by the young too as there are 'happiness gems' for one and all. I loved the cartoons too. It's a 'one stop' guide for living a happy life and truly a 'feel good' book.

Dr.Chandrasekaran, R. Former Professor, Madras Medical College, Chennai.

Mr Raman has brought out the various facets of life of seniors with empathy, narrating experiences including his own, blending humour, all of which make reading "Joyful Seniors..." joyful. Quotes from various luminaries give a feel of reading several great books from one. I am sure the book will receive lots of accolades from the readers and will be cherished for its content.

Mr.Gopalakrishnan, R. CEO, The Mindworks; Former Director, Tata Sons.

Congratulations Sri.Raman on your new book "Joyful Seniors". You are actively thinking, being responsive to other people's needs. The book is very easy to read, and potentially helpful for those who concede that they need help! My take is – 'As a couple ages, they must continue to work on their marriage and avoid the pitfalls of taking their marriage for granted. The great secret is not to treat all disasters as incidents, and not to treat incidents as disasters'

Ms.Jemima Young, Seven Hills, London on Behalf of Leena Nair, Unilever CHRO, London:

"We live in a world which is constantly changing and where opportunities are open to everyone - regardless of age. To find happiness, we need to ensure we put our individual purpose at the heart of our approach to daily life. Raman's book offers invaluable foresight into how to search for purpose, happiness and ensure learning is always a lifelong process"

Mr. Madvesh, C.K. Former Country Manager, MSD Agvet, Merck & Co.

I would term 'Joyful Seniors' as a 'Magnum Opus' due to its extensive and authentic research, covering every aspect of life of a senior. It's a guide for elders to live with independence, dignity, self respect, emotional and intellectual well being. On the 'taboo' topics, viz., Death and Sex, Mr. Raman has offered so many new insights that I read them repeatedly. In essence, it is an 'Encyclopaedia on Geriatrics'

Mr.Narayan, S, IAS. Former Finance Secretary, Government of India:

Surely 'Joyful Seniors' *is a window to leading a healthy and happy retired life, spreading good cheer all around. It's a welcome reading to all seniors. Mr Raman himself is an example of what he preaches - always of good cheer and eager to help others. It would be well to just try to be like him.*

Padmasri Dr.Natarajan, V.S. Founder & Chairman of Dr.V.S. Natarajan Geriatric Foundation, Chennai.

As a practicing Geriatrician, and one who is actively engaged with several elders on a day-to-day basis, I offer my compliments to Mr. S.V. Raman for writing such a useful ready reckoner. I am also glad to have read it and strongly recommend that all seniors do a deep reading. Mr. S.V.Raman with his zest for life, keen observations has touched upon variety of topics. I was pleasantly surprised that he has covered important topics including 'Polypharmacy' and hazards of 'self medication' which I have been always strongly advocating.

Dr. Raghavender Rao, Orthopaedic Surgeon.

"Joyful Seniors" is the most beautiful and interesting book. Words fail me in describing Raman's painstaking effort in bringing out this monumental write up, with thought provoking illustrations, while the graphics are brilliant. I have nothing to add as he has dealt all the topics thoroughly and imaginatively.

Dr.Sekhar, K. Former Director General, DRDO, Ministry of Defence:

'Joyful Seniors' is a must read and an excellent reference book to be kept handy to refer to during times of difficulties. Since, like a breath of fresh air it dispels many preconceived and unfounded notions, analyses touchy issues such as romance, sex, religion and death, with objectivity and sensitivity. Very interesting delineation has been done on spirituality and religiosity, highlighting their commonalities and significant differences. All the other subjects too are approached in an orderly manner based on experiences and excellent articles.

Mr. Shankar, Krish. Group Head – Human Resources, Infosys:

Raman's book fills a much-needed gap. It will help seniors to become more aware of likely issues, get tips on how to face them, prevent committing costly mistakes, and help them lead a safe and secure life. He has put this book together after studying various experiences - the beauty of the book is its comprehensive nature and its simple style, so that it can be beneficial for all seniors.

Happiness – Mine, Yours, Theirs

Just as some producers make profits even before releasing their movies, my happiness increased due to insights gathered while writing this book – even before it's published.

I am confident that you too would gain more happiness out of this book.

More importantly, you and I together will be adding happiness to the needy seniors – since all the profits from the sale of this book will be donated for their wellbeing.

S.V. Raman
Author

Queries, Answers and More

While doing research to write this book, I had a few doubts, and also faced some queries from others with whom I interacted. These are given below with my clarifications and answers so that the reader is clear before progressing to the main content.

Seniors know all, so what's the need for this book?

Yes, it's likely that majority of seniors would have read most topics. Those who haven't, might raise doubts like "Can I learn anything new at this age?" Some might ask "What's the use now?"

Given below are the various possible scenarios that justify why anyone, whatever is the age, can benefit with more happiness after reading this book.

- ***Read but Forgot!*** It is possible that the topics would have been read over an extended period, in different formats, from varied sources, but by now forgotten. This book offers the opportunity to read again and recollect.

- ***'Last and final call':*** There are some who would have read as well as remember everything, but don't practice all – like my knowledgeable friend (age 70, height 165 Cms, weight 115 Kgs.) who confessed that in the last fifteen years, he had neither went for a walk nor had any health checkups. And then another who has strained his relationships with family and friends and now in misery. For persons like them, this book can act as the 'last and final call', to make amends by putting into practice the recommendations to lead a more joyful life.

- ***Clarity and Reinforcement:*** Often, doubts arise if what one does (or doesn't) is correct; besides one may also would like to seek reinforcement. This book can help them on both these issues.

- ***'I am not alone':*** While facing many challenges, a senior could feel threatened by a doubt: 'Am I the only one to suffer this?' The numerous case studies could offer solace, besides offering possible ways to overcome them.

- ***Coping with changes:*** In just about couple of decades, significant and rapid changes have occurred in the lives of everyone. These have been identified, analysed and possible solutions presented for managing them in a better manner.

- ***New Findings:*** Many beliefs of the past have been proved wrong by new research. The reader now has the opportunity to become aware of the facts.

- ***'Taboo' topics:*** There have been some subjects, such as Sex and Death, which many shy away from. These have been detailed in this book, giving an opportunity to overcome apprehensions and fears about such topics.

- ***Authenticity:*** It has become common to receive fake information via various media. To avoid that, this book is well researched, and only authentic information from reliable sources is given. All the true stories are bona fide. Reviews by eminent personalities from diverse fields offer further credibility.

- ***Joyful to read:*** A book on joy should be a joy to read, isn't it? Hence, following features are incorporated: higher fonts for effortless reading; simple words and short sentences; bullet points for ease of understanding; summary at the end of every chapter for a quick recap; 'Good News' for every section to spread hope; quotes from eminent persons to inspire; cartoons, and wit in the narrative for humour - all of which run throughout the book, till the very end.

How to derive maximum benefit from this book?

- Being 'Open-Minded'. It means: willingness to learn; not to oppose any idea without careful consideration.

- Reading with a belief that increasing joy is in your control, and a conviction that you would make it happen.

- Doing introspection as you read. You may highlight lines/passages that create a strong impact. Later, reflect on them.

- Put learning to practice. Test. Then review.

A few other points to note

- The word 'Children' refers to adult offspring of elderly parents.

- In the true stories, names and places are omitted for confidentiality.

- Certain observations and recommendations are the opinion of the author, to which a reader may disagree – that could be expected. However, if a reader feels hurt, the author conveys his regret.

- Readers are welcome to share their views via email: soraiyurvraman @gmail.com. Please write 'Joyful Seniors' on the subject line.

HEALTH OF BODY & MIND

"Body and Mind are intricately interconnected. So each and every thought and feeling has effect on each and every cell in the body. Hence, they affect ageing – positively or negatively, as the case may be"

– Dr.Deepak Chopra, M.D, (B: 1946 Physician and Spiritualist), in 'Ageless Body, Timeless Mind'

"Youth is not a time of life, but a state of mind.

It is a matter of strength of the will, quality of imagination and predominance of courage.

It is possible that such qualities exist more in a man of 60 than a boy of 20.

Because, nobody grows old by mere years but due to giving up purpose in life, hope and ideals"

– Adapted from quote by Samuel Ullman (1840/1924, Humanitarian & poet)

AGE IS NOT A SINGLE NUMBER

Actually each one has not one but three ages, which are:

    i.   Chronological

    ii. Biological

    iii. Psychological

These are elaborated below:

i. Chronological age

This is the number of years from the birth date. However, due to the increased life expectancy, improved health services, it is classified into following 3 phases:

Age 60 to 70 is now called young - old, while, 71 to 80 as old – old, and 81 and above as older old.

The Chronological age cannot be changed (falsification of birth certificate is not considered), while the other two can, as detailed further.

ii. Biological age

Over the years, every human body undergoes numerous physiological changes, such as: degeneration of cells; fall in efficiency in digestion and respiration; reduction in bone mass; weakening of muscles and joints;

increased imbalance; deterioration in the senses; weakened nervous system, reduced immunity etc.

However, the World Health Organization (WHO) states *"there is no specific age that can be termed as 'old age', because some 80 year-olds have similar or even better fitness in both physical and mental capacities compared to some who are just 20 year-olds"*.

An interesting insight related to above is given in the book 'Ageless Body, Timeless Mind', by Dr. Deepak Chopra, which is: *"Most bodies are similar around age 20. But by the age 70, everybody is unique, mainly due to life style habits.* For instance, some angina patients with blockage in a single artery become disabled, whereas, there are people with multiple blockages who have run marathons"

From above it is evident that the Biological age, which is based on one's health and fitness levels, varies from person to person.

The good news: *Anyone, including seniors, can make amends, and slow down biological ageing. It is never too late. These are detailed below:*

Life style to slow down biological ageing

(Sources: 'Foods That Harm, Foods That Heal 'by Reader's Digest. WebMD. Talk by Prof. Mathew Walker, Professor of Neuroscience, Berkeley. IKIGAI –Japanese Secret to a Long and Happy Life):

Healthy Food Habits:

- Balanced diets (avoid excess carbohydrates & limit calories).

- Maximise intake of varieties of vegetables and fruits.

- Consume adequate amount of Macronutrients in larger quantities (protein, carbohydrates & fat); Micronutrients in smaller quantities (vitamins, minerals, enzymes, essential fatty acids and amino acids).

- Intake of required level of fiber.

- Hydrated body – drinking adequate water/fluids

- Chewing the food thoroughly ('drink solids, eat liquids')

- Stomach never above 80% full.

- Eat around the same time - every day.

- Manage body weight.

- Limit consumption of alcohol and caffeine.

Other Recommended Habits:

- Take prescribed medicines as per Doctor's instructions.

- Regular fitness regime, covering the following seven elements.

  1. Agility

  2. Balance

  3. Flexibility

  4. Motor skills

  5. Muscular strength

  6. Reflex

  7. Stamina

- Recent research reveals that *'ageing begins from feet, followed by legs, and then move upwards to heart and brain'*. So brisk walking is a must. However, those with medical conditions should consult their Physician before starting any new fitness activity, particularly after any serious illness or surgery.

- Never sit continuously for more than 45 minutes - get up, stretch, move, walk for 5 to 10 minutes.

- Get adequate sleep - 6 to 8 hours.

- Receive sun shine - 30 to 45 minutes.

- Regular bowel movement

- Maintain personal hygiene

- Get periodic medical checkups including dental, eye, ear etc.

- Correct Breathing – always

- No smoking

Brain: How to slow its ageing

(Sources: 'The Wisdom Paradox', by Elkhonon Goldberg. 'Use your Brain to change your age 'by Daniel Amen, M.D. 'Healthy Ageing', WebMD. "The Brain – The Story of You", by David Eagleman. 'www.lifeadvancer.com'. The Mayo Clinic):

Good News: According to recent studies, human brain has the following capabilities, many of which were unknown earlier (However, to derive these benefits, the brain has to be exercised well, and the recommended habits and life style, described earlier need to be followed).

- ***Neurogenesis:*** Brain can keep developing new neurons, pathways and circuits throughout one's life time. This capability can not only slow down ageing, but also can reverse ageing. In certain functions and cases, the brain could perform even better than in the past.

- ***Pattern recognition:*** This is the capability of the mind, which compensates a weakening brain, by utilising intuition based decision making. In such cases, those decisions are made not only quicker but also with lesser effort.

- ***Cognitive expertise:*** This refers to numerous case studies where seniors have undertaken complex, high level responsibilities, and executed them successfully, in diverse fields, including in art, science, engineering, politics, statesmanship etc. Many have achieved their peak fame/highest recognition at advanced age. A few examples are:

  - Johann Goethe (1749-1832) - his most acclaimed work was done when he was 83.

  - Allan Greenspan (B: 1926) was the Chairman of Federal Reserve, USA, from age 61 to 80.

  - Dr. Chandrasekhar (1910/1995) was awarded Nobel Prize when he was 73.

  - E. Sreedharan (B: 1932), was the Managing Director of the Delhi Metro between his age 63 and 80. From 83 till 86, he was a member of the UN's High Level Advisory Group on Sustainable Transport.

- ***Cognitive reserve:*** It is the brain's ability to take over the functions of other damaged tissues, so that a person may not feel any difference in his abilities.

- ***Auto rewiring:*** The brain has the intelligence and resource, which comes into action when a part of a body weakens or loses its function. In such instances, the brain rewires itself to compensate that loss - either totally or partly. For example, in a study of 110 persons with Dementia, though their brain tissues were damaged, yet there was no loss in cognitive functions (thinking, reasoning etc.).

- ***Improved selective memory:*** Contrary to earlier belief that all of brain's abilities decline after early 20's, new findings reveal that some types of memory can improve throughout life, such as - ability to recall concepts and facts

Recommended Habits to Enhance Brain Power

To get benefits of the above mentioned capabilities of the brain, one has to do the following regularly:

- **Be:** Childlike - curious, explore, laugh, and open to new ideas
- **Develop**: New skills & Interests, such as learning a new language, playing musical instruments, cooking, gardening, dancing etc
- **Do:** Yoga, Meditation, Tai chi, Prayers, Aerobic exercises etc
- **Get**: Body massage frequently.
- **Have:** Fun. Be cool.
- **Involve**: Do voluntary work for the community/needy
- **Make:** Love, safe sex
- **Network:** Maintain existing, and create new relationships
- **Play:** Outdoor & Indoor games to enhance alertness, memory etc.
- **Read:** Novels, books of varied genre, by different authors.
- **Solve**: Cross word puzzles, Sudoku etc.
- **Socialise**: Meet and chat with people who spread positivity.

- **Undergo:** New experiences

- **Write:** Diary of daily activities, insights, anecdotes, short stories etc

---

Healthy Habits to prevent entry of toxins

Toxins are substances that cause harm to cells, the basic building blocks in the body. They also interfere with functioning of organs, leading to diseases, resulting in accelerated ageing. Hence, following actions need to be taken:

Entry of toxins through various sources:

- Cooking/Reheating:

  - Via non-stick items like tava, aluminium utensils, microwave oven.

- Consumption

  - Via food that contain:

    o High level of salt, sugar, 'chilly'.

    o Processed white sugar, refined cooking oil, refined carbohydrates etc.

    o Hydrogenated fats. Aerated drinks. Colas Processed/Canned food. White bread. Sweets. Biscuits. Ready mixes.

- Packing/storage:

  - Thermocol

  - Plastic bags/pouches, including take- away.

- Air:

  - Items that contain synthetic materials, e.g. rugs, curtains, carpets, mattress etc.

  - Agabatti, Dhoop, Air/Room fresheners, Mosquito repellents, Sprays/Aerosol, Mothballs. Furniture using particle board

- Body:

  - Personal care products that use harmful chemicals, such as in tooth paste, soap, shampoo, cream, lotions, hair dye etc.

Prevention of entry of toxins:

- Maximise consumption of organic food

- Use only naturally made Ayurvedic, Organic products

- Drink pure water in adequate quantity.

- Limit or avoid usage of perfumes, deodorants

- Never indulge in self medication

Longevity

Long life has been always considered a boon. 'Dheergayusu Bhava' is a common blessing an elder gives to anyone younger.

According to a TED talk (April 2017 by Ms. Susan Pinker), on 'Lifestyle', the two major factors to long life are:

i. Genetics: 25% (Not in one's control and a minor factor).

ii. Lifestyle : 75% (In one's control and a major contributor)

Susan focuses on healthy social life - close, quality relationships with family, friends, relatives, neighbours and the community.

Those interactions should be predominantly 'Face to Face', with eye contacts, handshakes, hugs etc. (the last two exempted till resolution of Covid 19). This means digital, virtual interaction like What's app, Facebook, Instagram, texting, Internet chat etc. are *not* as effective as personal interaction.

Another dimension is offered by Norman Cousin, in 'Anatomy of Illness', quoting research on very old people across the world, and concluding that longevity is closely related to the following three factors:

i.   Frugal, but well-balanced diet

ii. Vigorous and continual physical activity

iii. Meaningful purpose in life.

The book 'IKIGAI – The Japanese Secret to long and happy life' based on studies also reinforces the same three reasons listed above. While the first two are quite clear, the third factor - meaningful purpose needs some elaboration. It is essentially beyond any self interest; an active involvement in social, community affairs.

This is further corroborated by Pablo Casals, Spanish cellist and musician (1876/1973), who was active till his end; he once shared "Anyone can do something for peace, since each one has inside him a basic decency and goodness, and hence can offer something to the world"

Similar sentiment was expressed by Albert Schweitzer (1875/1965, French humanitarian, Physician and Musician), who lived a life of action in public service till he died at 90. He once told his staff "I have no intention of dying, so long as I can do things. And if I do things, there is no need to die. So I will live for long time".

———•—●—•———

iii. Psychological age

This is a person's sense of wellbeing.

Significance of Psychological age is explained by Deepak Chopra, M.D in 'Ageless Body, Timeless Mind'. He observes "Two patients of stroke, both in mid 50's, with identical medical conditions, could have vastly different recovery time due to Psychological factors"

Good News: Research reveals that majority of the factors that decide Psychological age can be controlled; that it is never too late to slow down Psychological age too.

———•—●—•———

Factors that affect Psychological age are:

1. Physical Health

2. Personality Traits

3. Behaviour

4. Mind Discipline

5. Managing Stress

6. Financial Health.

7. Relationships.

8. Spirituality.

9.   Romance, Love & Sex.

10. Joyfulness

While the Physical health (Biological ageing) has been already dealt in the earlier chapter, others are detailed in this and subsequent chapters.

—◆—

Personality Traits

It would be useful to recall the five personality traits (abbr. OCEAN), as below:

1. **Openness:** Attitude to learn, experience new things. Its opposite is 'a closed mind' – an attitude of 'I know everything'.

2. **Conscientiousness:** Organised; Committed; Dependable; Trustworthy. The opposites are: Disorderly; Non - trustworthy.

3. **Extroversion:** Sociable; Friendly; Keen to meet, interact with people. Its opposites are: Introversion, Shyness.

4. **Agreeableness:** Warm hearted; Empathetic; Co-operative. Its opposites are: Quarrelsome; Insensitive (to feelings of others).

5. **Neuroticism:** Poor emotional stability; Extreme mood swings; Possessing significant level of negativity (e.g. fear, envy, jealousy, guilt and anger).

Changes in personality traits in seniors: Past research had revealed that by age of thirty, one's Personality gets fixed. However several recent research findings have proved that wrong as detailed below.

American Psychological Association, issue of July 2003, observes that 'most people's personalities evolve throughout their lives, though it may not be on all the 5 traits.

An article in The Time magazine, titled 'Science of us', Nov. 2014, reports that "with a strong intention and conscious efforts (internal process), change in most personality traits is possible, at any age. This also means that traits cannot be taught (i.e. external pressure would not work)".

More insights come from 'Psychology Today', by Dr.Vitelli, who observes that personality changes can occur, including for old people, depending on new life experiences or life-changing events. He further states "as our lives change, so do our personalities".

A woman (60+), who used to be trust worthy and composed till her mid 40's, became non-trustworthy and neurotic from her early 50's, after series of setbacks in money and relationships.

My wife and I were shy and introverted till our mid 30's. Then, changes occurred in our work as well as in the living environment, and we gradually became extroverts. Besides, my Openness and Agreeableness have also changed, for better, after my retirement.

———•———

On behaviour and true stories among seniors

Behaviour can be taught and learnt (i.e. unlike personality). As years pass-by, behavioural changes happen, including in seniors.

There are two reasons for recounting below some true stories on possible behavioural changes – firstly to increase awareness among seniors; secondly to educate family members/caregiver to become more empathetic.

Aggression: On many occasions, elders, who used to be calm, even docile in the past, begin to behave aggressively and abusive. Often, this happens during illness, hospitalisation, disability etc. It could be also due to side effects of certain medications. During those times, the spouse/care giver too could experience stress. However, in majority of the cases, after getting cured, the person returns to their earlier normal behaviour.

Arrogance: Some who have enjoyed enormous power, perquisites during their work life, behave the same way even after retirement.

An administrator of a high end SCL lamented that some residents behave as if they are still in power, for example, intentionally violating the community rules.

Attention Seeking: With growing age, some seek attention. One common technique is to complain about pain, illness, uneasiness etc., with the intention to get noticed and cared for.

A friend (55) told that he keeps 'Gems' (as a placebo) and whenever his mother (85) complains, he gives one to her and she stops lamenting.

Childish: As years pass by, a tendency to behave childish (silly, foolish etc.) could occur.

When I was 65, I visited a garden in Singapore and noticed a 'toy' python on a tree. Believing that it was a gimmick, I went very close to take a Selfie. Then, on the mobile screen, I noticed the snake's tongue coming out for a split second. To my horror, I realised that the snake was alive. My wife, who was witnessing the incident, admonished me "stop behaving childish".

Denial mode: It is not uncommon that though the body begins to develop limitations, the mind often refuses to accept.

A man (90) fell down, when a scooter passed close to him. The rider, a middle aged man, stopped, said apologetically "Sorry Uncle". The elder, struggling to get up, retorted "Don't dare to call me uncle. I am not that old."

Disproportionate reaction: Even for petty incidents, some over react, as if it is a matter of life or death.

Once, after I had occupied a seat in an aircraft, an elderly person came and yelled at me for occupying the seat assigned to him.

Imaginary fears: Some tend to imagine all kinds of scary scenarios and get frightened.

A woman (70+) refused a package from a courier. Since the sender's name was not familiar, she imagined that it was a 'parcel bomb'. Later her daughter called and informed that it was a gift from her, but to make it a surprise, she sent it in her friend's name.

Inept Talk: This is done without thinking about the consequences.

A friend was busy making arrangements for the wedding of his daughter, when his uncle (75) called "I read a message in What's App that there could be a 'bandh' on the day of the wedding. Are you planning to cancel the event?" My friend was angry with that insensitive talk.

Insecurity: Many, even if in good health, feel threatened to be alone, even at home. So, they insist that a family member should always be present.

A neighbour told that whenever he goes out of his home, leaving his mother (88) alone, she would sulk, sit in a corner, and refuse to talk to him.

Importance to dress & looks: While some retired men lose interest in these things, most women seem to continue to give importance, while a few go to extremes.

When I visited a retired CEO, I was shocked by his cluttered look. I enquired if he was unwell, to which he explained "No, I am ok. Since there are no more board meetings, I don't care about my dress and looks".

During one of my morning walks, I noticed an elderly woman wearing a pair of high heal footwear and walking briskly. I suggested that she should wear proper walking shoes, to which she replied "but that won't suit this dress".

Losing confidence: As years pass by, some tend to lose confidence in many skills. This seems to increase rapidly with age.

In the year 2000, when I was 50 and living in Netherlands, I used to drive to unknown destinations, though there was no GPS then. Now, I would not dare to do that even with GPS. Instead, I would opt for a package tour.

Losing interest: With increasing age, a few tend to lose interest in everything.

I was chatting up with a man (91), who shared that till he was 75, he used to read, travel and attend all social events. "Now, nothing motivates me" he said.

Men becoming more emotional: According to 'Psychology Today', men cry more as they get older, due to following reasons: Men are more likely to have suppressed emotions of the past as they were expected to be strong in any situation and never cry. However, when they become old, they are less concerned about that 'image', and so cry easily.

Other possible factors are: Hormonal changes; Loneliness; Health issues; Side effects of medications etc.

When I was 67, I spent a month with my granddaughter. While leaving, I suppressed my tears, but cried immediately after entering the cab, shocking the driver and embarrassing my wife

Obstinacy: Throughout the Covid Pandemic there was continual dissemination to wear masks and keep social distancing. Yet, many educated and some with serious health issues have consistently refused to follow those rules.

Over anxious: Some envisage all kinds of 'worst case scenarios', and take 'corrective actions'. For instance, ahead of any travel, they would complete their packing and ready to depart a few days in advance; a few pester other family members to do so. This anxiety seems to have reached a new high during the Covid 19 – a few had shut all the windows after reading 'forwards' in What's App.

A woman (70+) gets tensed if her husband is out of her sight for more than ten minutes – even when both are inside their apartment.

A man (85+), living alone, whenever stepping out of his apartment, even for short duration, carries a bag containing bank pass books, cheque books, passport, PAN & Aadhar cards and the keys of ward robes as he is afraid that these could be stolen.

Pessimism: It's usual to hear elders complaining about the younger generation, blaming them for 'degeneration of culture, erosion of morality' etc. Ironically, such statements have been repeatedly made in every generation for centuries.

"The children now love luxury, have bad manners, contemptuous to authority, and show no respect to their parents ....." said Socrates, Greek Philosopher, twenty four centuries ago!

Quarrelsome: It is not uncommon to watch couples/siblings – all seniors – quarrel frequently. This is often mis understood by on lookers as lack of love between them, but that does not seem so in majority of instances.

A couple (both 70+) squabble as a routine, but those who know them well are aware that the reason for it is the extra ordinary care for each other.

Risk aversion: Some of the routine tasks done by youngsters appear risky for the aged.

Many elders are afraid to use credit cards, avail Net banking, do on-line shopping etc., due to possibility of 'getting cheated and losing all the money'.

Self- centeredness: .A few behave as if the whole world is there to serve them.

In a housing complex, a lady (80+) demanded that a post box should be installed, at her apartment block. She was explained that very few write letters, and was asked 'How often you write letters?" to which she replied 'once in six months'.

Stubbornness: Some wouldn't realise that what is being told is in their interest.

Father of my friend (75+), refused to move to live with his son, stubbornly living alone in his ancestral house in a village without adequate health care. Later he passed away for want of immediate medical attention.

Suspicion: Suspecting everyone and everything is not unusual.

A relative told me that as a goodwill gesture he used to visit his neighbour (84) who was living alone. After a few occasions, the elder began to suspect and told him brusquely "You don't come. When I am dead, you will know"

Worrisome: Tendency to worry on which one has neither control nor responsibility is another issue.

A lady (80+) kept worrying about education of her great grandson (3) since, he with his parents were moving to Spain where English is not the medium of instruction.

In another instance, a 75 year old shared his concern on how his granddaughter (7) would manage her life due to ever increasing cost of living.

To reiterate, above incidents illustrating odd behaviours are shared with the sole purpose to increase awareness.

It is also important to note that any sudden, significant behavioural changes should be taken seriously, as they could be symptoms of depression, dementia etc. In such cases, it is important that a Geriatrician be consulted.

⎯ ◆ ⎯

Mind Discipline

This is third in the list that affects Psychological ageing.

Mind and Body: Understanding the connection between mind and body is crucial for happiness. In the past, many, particularly the West, believed that the body and mind are two separate entities, and that the mind is superior to the body. However, long ago, Patanjali's Yoga Sutra stated that the mind is not something inside the head, but is a function, an activity, and so all pervasive. Later, the study on the evolution has supported this by revealing the intricate and inseparable interconnection - that every cell in the body has acquired the intelligence gathered over millions of years.

The second factor that needs understanding is about feelings and emotions. Although these two are often used without distinction, they are quite different as explained by Dr.Sarah Mckay, Neuro scientists 'Emotions arise from the body; it's a lower level response; based on instincts. Hence emotions are quite similar for all humans and are usually temporary. On the contrary feelings arise from the mind, it is a higher level response; unique to every individual; last for long period - even whole lifetime. In spite of these differences, emotion and feeling are closely interconnected because body and mind are. So, when feelings are triggered by emotions, the vice versa also happens'.

The third factor is the large difference in the duration of happy and unhappy memories. Most people would have noticed that un happy memories lasts much longer, combined with stronger feelings even for decades compared to happy ones, which are shorter and with lesser impact. This is explained in 'The Neurochemistry of Positive Conversations', by Dr.Richard D. Glaser, who observed that unpleasant memories produce cortisol, the 'stress' hormone to fight any threat (real or imaginary), which lasts longer. On the contrary, the 'happiness hormone' such as Oxytocin, is short-lived.

Above findings have significance, particularly to elders, since many have free time to brood over the past.

Managing Stress

This the fourth in the list of Psychological ageing

Stress is the way body/mind react to anything that is *perceived* as a threat – it could be a thought, situation, emotion or feeling – real or imaginary.

It is vital to be aware that a person's ability to manage stress deteriorates with time.

Major causes of stress: *(Sources: Harvard Women's Health. "25 Things you need to know about Stress…". Reader's Digest Jan. 2017).*

- Loss/Bereavement (death of spouse/family member)

- Major change(s) in life (retirement, relocation of home)

- Trauma (serious illness, hospitalisation, disability)

- Dependence on others (for money, doing routine activities)

- Inability to meet expectations (from family & others).

- Illness/Injury (resulting in pain, disability)

- No purpose in life (too much idling)

- Loneliness (lack of social, face to face interactions)

- Lack of good, adequate sleep (causing restlessness, anxiety)

- Poor/Unhealthy habits (addictions)

- Sedentary life style (inadequate exercise)

- Pessimism (negativity)

- Clutter (accumulation of unwanted things)

———•●•———

Tips to manage stress

Intuition ('Gut Feel'): It's the ability to understand something instinctively, which helps in stress relief through correct decision making, problem solving, with less efforts. Studies show that elders have higher capability to use intuition due to long experience backed by knowledge, Since women have better intuition, husbands can (continue to) delegate decision making to their wives.

———•●•———

Other tips to manage stress:

- Watch thoughts. Reduce them through meditation, yoga etc.

- Identify the source of stress; then self- assure that it can be resolved.

- Take frequent deep breaths. Do Pranayam. Pray. Practice Silence

- Slow down Biological ageing (detailed earlier)

- Plan in advance to minimise uncertainties, crisis like situations.

- Get rid of common stressors with below mentioned practices:

  ○ Learn to utilise useful features of smart phone such as:

    - Store: Things to do. Items to buy etc.

    - Set alarms (e.g. for intake of medicines; buying them in advance; appointment with Doctor; scheduled tests etc.)

    - Be prepared for emergencies (details in another chapter).

  ○ Automate bill payments (e.g. electricity, mobile, cable TV etc.)

  ○ Keep spares of frequently used but likely to be misplaced items - chargers, spectacles, house keys etc.

  ○ Keep minimum number of credit, debit cards, bank accounts

  ○ Segregate and maintain all documents (medical, tax, bills, receipts, guarantee cards etc.)

  ○ Maintain good housekeeping: Cultivate a habit of keeping medicines, mobile, keys, spectacles, files etc. in the same, visible place.

———•———

Chronological, Biological and Psychological

In the above illustration, which is adapted from Dr Deepak Chopra's 'Ageless Body and Timeless Mind', the Chronological age of both Sunil (walking) & Ramesh (sitting) are 60. But their effective ages are: 35 (Sunil) and 80 (Ramesh), due to different Biological age (habits and life style) and Psychological age (behaviour, traits & spirituality).

Summary on Health of Body & Mind:

- ✓ *Ageing can be slowed down, and in some cases, even reversed*

- ✓ *It is never too late to change one's life style, behaviour and attitude to improve health of body & mind*

EMERGENCY PREPAREDNESS, SAFETY, SECURITY & PREVENTION OF ABUSE

Being prepared for any emergency will improve the ability to offer as well as receive help

— The Red Cross

Seniors can live safely, securely, and prevent getting abused, by behaving responsibly and learning to be assertive.

— Various Studies

PREPARATION FOR POSSIBLE EMERGENCIES

Emergency is any unplanned, unexpected situation or an incident, often serious, that require immediate action. Though emergency cannot be predicted, one can be prepared to manage it well, so as to minimise the impact. This has higher relevance to seniors as they are more vulnerable and so at a higher risk; particularly so if they live away from their Children.

So here are the important tips to plan and manage emergencies:

1. Store in mobile as well as write and display in a prominent place at home, the following important contact numbers:

   - Children's

   - Family physician

   - Nearest Hospital

   - Neighbours. Friend/Relative (living nearby)

   - Ambulance. Fire. LPG leaks. Jurisdictional Police Station

2. Keep at easily accessible, visible place the medical files that contain: medical history, recent reports and prescriptions; list of allergic substances; blood group; medical insurance etc.

3. Cash: Keep it separately to be used only for emergency purposes.

4. Credit Card/Debit card with reasonable balance amount.

5. Photo ID & Address Proof (Aadhar/Voter ID/Driving licence/ Passport)

6. Before undertaking any travel, share details of itinerary (train/ flight/hotel etc.) with Children/Neighbour/Close friend.

Prevention of injuries due to fall.

(Source: "A Senior's Guide to Fall Prevention and Healthy Living", Roxanne Reynolds)

For seniors

The 1ˢᵗ fall is probably the beginning of old age.

The 2ⁿᵈ fall could possibly be the end of old age.

Some useful information about fall:

- Fall is the most common cause of injury

- Fall is the biggest cause of hospitalisation and death for those above 75.

- Of all the falls, 55% occur at home. Most of it in the bathroom.

- It is possible to prevent falls.

Causes of fall due to health conditions

- Low/High blood pressure.

- Poor body balance.

- Poor eye sight.

- Poor blood sugar control.

- Dizziness including side effects of medications.

- Epilepsy/Other issues related to nervous system.

- Vertigo.

- Vitamin deficiency - B6, B12 & D.

- Osteoporosis.

- Dementia/Parkinson's.

- Fear of fall (it increases if one had a fall in the past).

- Poor concentration (lost in thoughts, not noticing things around).

- Excess consumption of alcohol.

Causes of fall due to unsafe conditions & behaviours

- Poor housekeeping including wet floor, objects on the way.

- Multi tasking (doing more than one job at a time)

- Absence or poor condition of: hand railings, steps.

- In bath & toilet, absence of: anti skid flooring, grab bars, proper sloping, shower curtains etc.

- Unsafe (slippery, curly, too many) mats, carpets, rugs.

- Inadequate lighting.

- Use of foldable/broken items: E.g. ladders, stools, chairs, tables

- Improper clothing/dress

- Ill fitting footwear

Awareness of above causes and taking preventive, corrective actions will reduce chances of fall, injury and even death.

Prevention of shock, injury, death due to electrical faults

- Check provision of Earth Leak Circuit Breaker (ELCB) which prevents shock due to faulty gadgets, wiring etc.

- Ensure no joints in wires/cables.

- Don't overload by connecting several gadgets in one socket.

- Use only 3 Pin plugs with equipment body connected to the earth.

- Employ only qualified persons to work on electricity

- Don't operate switches with moist hands/wet floors.

Prevention of dangers with secured living

- Elders living away from Children should avoid living alone in independent houses or in isolated locations. Instead, they can choose to live in –apartments in housing complexes, well equipped Seniors community living with 24 x 7 security, Intercom, access control etc.

- If that's not feasible, install video cameras hooked to Internet (so Children can monitor). Where feasible, utilise home automation like motion detectors, wearable emergency button with messaging facility etc – cost of these have dropped significantly over the years. Studies have shown that these drastically reduce crime.

- Be friendly and in touch with neighbours.

- If living alone, talk to Children/relative/friend/neighbour every day.

- Ensure mobile phone(s) is always fully charged and bills paid.

- Install emergency push button(s) to alert security.

- While employing any service provider (e.g. maid, driver, assistant), hire them only from licensed service providers with police verification. Keep a copy of their photo ID and address proofs.

- Expensive items, such as jewellery and cash, as well as credit/debit cards, cheque books, bank pass books etc. should be kept securely.

- Never discuss money matters in presence of service staff.

- When any repair/service person comes, verify their ID before allowing entry. As far as possible, allow them only during day time.

———— •◆•• ————

Prevention of accidents due to fire

- Beware of/be away from any open flame like 'diya' used for 'puja'.

- If feasible use only induction stove(s). If LPG used, install gas leak alarm.

- Beware of fire due to electrical faults.

———— •◆•• ————

Prevention of abuse of Seniors

What constitutes an abuse? Any intentional, negligent act, which causes physical, emotional or mental stress, is termed as 'abuse'. Typical abuses are: verbal insult; physical beating; not providing food, shelter, safety, security; stealing; cheating etc.

Major reasons for abuse

Values and customs practiced over centuries, such as, respect, obedience to elders are getting eroded. In the past, elders had plenty of scope and opportunities to contribute to the family, by imbibing values, educating, guiding, advising, and sharing their wisdom. But that scope has reduced rapidly due to emergence of nuclear family; rapid advances of technology which facilitates easy availability of information mostly for free. Concurrently the knowledge and skills possessed by seniors are rapidly becoming obsolete. These reasons have gradually undermined the constructive role played by elders in the family for centuries.

Abuses are also accentuated by the growing number of elders due to increasing life expectancy. In India, the population of elders was 90 million in 2008 (8% of total), grew to 130 million by 2020 (10%), and by 2050, would rise to 340 million (20%).

According to Helpage India (a non profit organization for the aged), 50% of seniors face some form of abuse at home. And 98% of those who suffered refuse to file any police complaint.

And the pandemic has further worsened the situation due to strain in income and stress in relationships.

All of these indicate that increasing numbers of elders are likely to be abused in future too.

True stories of mental, physical, emotional abuse

Assault: I was of the opinion that this kind of abuse happens only in slums, indulged by drunken men till I heard a few first person accounts of such occurrences in educated, wealthy families too.

Cheating: This is done to grab cash, jewellery, house, land etc. owned by elders.

A youngster, living abroad, persuaded his mother in India to sell the ancestral house she was living, and asked her come and settle with him. She trusted him, sold the house and handed over the money. Son escorted mother to the airport, left her there, and flew away. She was later admitted to a home for destitute.

Exploitation: Financially dependent elderly parents are kept by their Children till they are useful, such as during pregnancy, bringing up the kids etc. Once the need ceases, the elderly parents are discarded.

Gender Bias: In well to do families as well as in Old Age Home (OAH), elderly women are preferred and easily get admitted, as they contribute in cooking, washing, housekeeping etc., while the men are usually considered of no use, don't get admitted easily and even ill treated.

Stress and Strain: A popular terminology is IAS - Indian Aaya Service, which refers to elderly parents serving their Children, during pregnancy, child birth, baby sitting, cooking and serving freshly prepared food, dropping/picking grand children to/from school and extra- curricular activities. While many elders seem to do it out of love, the others do out of compulsion. In the case of Children living abroad, the stress is manifold, which includes - long haul flights; dependence on Children to move around; limited opportunities to pursue interests, socialise; uncomfortable weather conditions etc. The elderly men seem to be in worse situation since many are not inclined to do the chores. As a consequence they get bored and desperately look forward to returning home.

In the second kind of abuse, it's the elderly fathers who are put under stress by their Children to manage the latter's fixed assets (house/

apartments/land etc) – again this is also more common among Children living abroad. The man has to run around for various jobs such as carrying out painting/carpentry/interiors; vacating old tenant, finding new tenant, payment of taxes, regularising property related documents etc.

The third kind of abuse is mental anguish, which is common to both the genders, wherein a grandchild is prevented from interacting with the grandparents. This happens to settle old scores between the Children and their elderly parents/In laws.

Selfishness: It is no longer uncommon to come across Children who keep only their personal interest in their minds.

A retiree wanted to continue to work to build his inadequate pension corpus. But his daughter living abroad prevented that as she wanted her mother's help during child birth and for the next two years. Though she needed services of only her mother, since her father can't be left alone in India, he was forced to stay abroad. After returning, he could not find any work. He was forced to sell his apartment located in the city to build retirement corpus and move to a rented place in a distant suburb.

Unaware: In a few instances, Children seem to be not conscious that they are causing stress, and they keep expecting same level of service from elders as was the case decades ago.

———•———

Self Inflicted Abuse

This may seem strange but many seniors, for various reasons, inflict abuse on themselves, which are avoidable. A few true stories follow:

Unwarranted stress: *A man (80+) was scampering for painting, fixing a tenant for an apartment owned by his daughter living abroad, in spite of her advice to get everything done by an agent. He explained "Agents take money and I would like to save for my daughter".*

Mind Set: Some of those who were poor in their younger days but became wealthy after their 40's/50's, continue their frugal life style.

An elderly couple became 'crorepati' after the man turned 60, but they continued to live the way they did in the past. The woman, inspite of frail health, would not hire a domestic help, continued to do all the household work by herself; her husband would walk under the hot sun, take the public transport to travel to far away destinations.

Creating rift: It is not uncommon that some elderly parents create misunderstanding between their own Children for inexplicable reasons.

An elder, while staying with her son would blame her daughter living elsewhere. And when she goes to live with that daughter, she would find faults with her son.

Naivety: Most seem to believe that their Children would never ever exploit or cheat them, that such things happen only to others.

Outdated customs: *A woman in early 40's shared that her widowed mother (85+), in poor health, refused to stay with her and reasoned with "our tradition is that once a daughter is given away in marriage, parents should never stay with her".*

Rivalry: *Some* elderly couples compete with each other as if they are sworn enemies. They frequently blame, accuse each other, even in front of their Children/Grand children, which destroys relationships.

Wasteful efforts: A friend (66) took lot of efforts and constructed a 3 storied house in his home town for himself and his two sons who had settled abroad. I asked him if his children have any plans to return to India, to which he replied 'I am not sure'. A few years later, against his wishes, he had to sell that building (with lot of efforts and incurring loss) to migrate and live with them.

———•◆•———

Hope for seniors

The United Nations (UN) has designated June 15 as the World Elder Abuse Awareness Day to create better understanding and reduce abuse. In India, from time to time, laws have been enacted to prevent abuse as summarised below:

1. The provision in the Constitution for justice in social, political, economic, equality of rights is applicable for elders also.

2. Social security is a joint responsibility of both Central & State governments.

3. The Hindu adoption and Maintenance Act, 1956, and Widow's right of inheritance are enacted to protect elders against abuse.

4. Criminal Procedure Code (CPC) and Indian Penal Code (IPC) have specific provisions to support elderly parents, and both son and daughter are responsible to maintain them.

5. Essence of Maintenance & Welfare of Parents and Senior Citizens Act 2007:

   • Mandates need based maintenance to the parents/grandparents from their children/grand children.

   • Tribunals are set up for quick settling of maintenance claims of elders.

- Mandates protection of life, property; better medical facilities; setting up Old Age Homes in every district.

- 'Integrated Program for Older Persons'(IPOP) provides financial assistances to maintain Old Age Homes run by the Government, NGO's and other local bodies.

- Most States as well as Central Government offer pension to the needy elders under various schemes.

However, with the trend of increasing numbers of seniors (mentioned earlier), it is unlikely that only the Governments and NGO's would be able to significantly improve their quality of life. Hence other socially conscious citizens, you and me, need to support the deprived elders with our time, efforts and money.

Reason why this author will be donating all the profits from sale of this book to the welfare of deprived elders.

Summary: Emergency, Safety, Security & Prevention of abuse

- ✓ **Being prepared helps to manage any emergency with less effort and stress.**

- ✓ **Safety, Security and Abuse of elders can be reduced by:**

  - o **Spreading more awareness with training on safe, responsible & assertive behaviour**

  - o **Society (you and me) taking more responsibility.**

MONEY MATTERS

Caution to seniors: Your Children may not contribute to your pension fund.

Reminder to Children: Your Parents are neither your ATM nor your banker.

IMPORTANCE OF MONEY

The Tamil saint and poet Avvaiyar (2nd century CE) sang "The worst misfortune in anyone's life is poverty in youth". However, if that sage were to be alive today, she might modify it as "The most terrible thing to happen to anyone is poverty in old age". That's because, in her times, elders were respected, obeyed and taken care of. It is no longer so.

Significance of ensuring adequacy and safeguarding money

- Money is among the most important factors for stress free life for anyone – that is known to all. But more so for any senior because, if he has not earned enough or loses, it would be difficult to regain, since, he may not possess all essential requirements – time, energy, opportunity, skill etc.

- Hence, it is essential for elders to be extra prudent and self sufficient till the end of their lives; not dependent upon anyone, including their Children - however loving and caring they are.

Based on the above, for seniors who are solely dependent on their Retirement Corpus (i.e. those with limited wealth), following are the recommendations:

- *Retirement Corpus (RC)* refers to the total wealth owned by a senior to meet all the 'essential 'expenses, till the demise of both.

- The total wealth can be classified as those which generate income and others which could bring capital appreciation/depreciation. Regular income sources include: Pension; PF/EPF; Deposits (banks/company); stocks/mutual funds; rentals etc. Other assets include: jewellery, land, motor vehicles etc.

- Income from RC should be sufficient to meet the following 'essential' needs: balanced food; comfortable, safe and secure accommodation; healthy lifestyle; medical expenses; spiritual pursuit; recreation; hobbies etc.

- RC should be adequate to cover not only the present but also the future needs taking into account depleting value of money (inflation, detailed later), higher medical expenses, other emergencies and increasing life expectancy.

- Bank accounts, deposits and other investments be preferably in either or survivor or jointly with spouse. Children could be the nominees and/or given in a Will after the demise of both the parents.

- RC should *not* be depleted, for frivolous expenses or offering loans etc.

- Transfer of ownership of the sole residence to Children to be done only after the demise of both, via a Will.

- PIN number and the respective Credit/Debit card together should never be kept together. Same is the case for Login Id and Pass words for Bank accounts.

- Credit Card is safer than Debit card, since, in the event of a fraud, one can block the credit card, lodge a complaint, and refuse to pay. That is not so in Debit card where money gets instantly deducted from the account.

- Automate the minimum payment due against credit card since outstanding amount attracts high interest charges.

- In the event of shortage of money, reverse mortgage is an option offered by many banks, where, money can be earned from own house, while living in it, till the demise of both. The income is based on its valuation. After the demise of the couple, the Bank would offer that house for sale as per the prevailing market rate to the Children. If that does not materialize, bank would sell to any other person and recover the money.

A senior's top most priority should be safeguarding wealth.

Significance of growing wealth, and related issues

It is not enough just to safeguard wealth, but is also necessary to grow it to meet the various risks which are detailed below:

- ***Longevity Risk***: As per Aegon Retirement Readiness Survey (2016), an Indian who is 60, can expect to live upto 82. This being an average figure, for monetary security, it is recommended that a person plans to live upto to 90. This is called Longevity Risk.

- **_Inflation Risk:_** This refers to continuous decrease in value of money (purchasing power) due to inflation, which would always exist. Given below is an example of how value of money gets reduced:

  i. Rs. 1 Lakh in 1984 is worth less than Rs.7500 in 2016

  ii. So if a person, aged 60 now spends Rs 30,000/month, then at age 90, he would need Rs 3 Lakhs/month to maintain the same quality of life (basis: 8% inflation/annum).

  In fact, the above estimate could be higher since the cost of services, such as assisted living, which one may need with advancing years, could be expected to be higher than 8 %, considered in the above working.

- **_Return vs. Risk:_** RC should not be invested in schemes that promises abnormally high returns compared to the market situation, since the rule is: 'high return always carries high risk'. For example, Co-Operative banks, Chit Funds, Credit societies, Private enterprises offer higher returns on fixed deposits compared to Nationalised banks, but the latter is considered safer.

- **Risk in seeking assistance**: To increase the wealth, while availing services (free or paid) from wealth/asset management persons, agents, distributors from banks or other agencies, extreme caution need to be exercised, since many of them are known to offer advice with a view to _maximise their income_ instead of the clients. Options to prevent such occurrences are: take support from Children/trustworthy friends or relatives; self education (at least on the fundamentals), getting second opinion etc.

- **Longer gestation period**: RC is also not recommended to be invested in fixed assets like land and building, since such investments could take 15 to 20 years to give significantly higher returns compared to other lower risk & lower return investments like Mutual Funds. Besides, not all investments in such fixed assets manage to offer even decent returns; it is also not unusual that investment in such assets is lost due to frauds

- **Review:** Make periodic review how RC and other investments perform.

- **Rich dad – Poor dad:** Some elders could be rich in assets, but poor in cash, as they lock too much money on non-cash generating assets, like huge house, vacant land, expensive jewellery, unrented premises etc. Some spend on assets that are expensive to maintain and depreciate fast like luxury cars. So, in spite of being 'rich', they live like 'poor' due to inadequate cash flow.

  A friend, who had worked abroad till retirement, on return, built a huge mansion in his hometown, spending most of his earnings on it. He is now forced to travel by train even to long distances as he doesn't have cash for air travel.

- **Money becoming a stressor:** Due to lethargy, procrastination or to save money on paying a Chartered Accountant, some keep delaying filing of income tax returns or don't take efforts to resolve outstanding issues. When they receive a Demand Notice from the Income Tax department with penalty, they become stressed, which could have been avoided.

  Continuing the past habit, some flaunt numerous credit/debit cards, not realising that more their numbers, higher the risks. For most, one or two credit/debit cards should be adequate.

- **Make money work:** Before retirement, most would have worked hard, sacrificed a lot to earn money for the welfare of their families. Post retirement, they should make that money work harder for their safety, health, comfort and happiness.

- **Be prepared:** Among many couples, money matters are managed by one - mostly by the husbands. To be prepared for any eventuality, at least basic information/training should be imparted and, all related documents and information should be kept in order and explained to spouse who is unaware of them, and Children kept informed . These include: land, house, taxes, pension, PPF, medical insurance, bank/DMAT accounts, FD's, lockers, loans (receivable/payable), utility bills etc.

Making a Will & Testament

Points to note: i) All seniors should prepare Will and if needed Testament while in good physical and mental health. ii) Hand written is also valid. iii) It should be certified by a medical practitioner iv) Also to be signed by two witnesses. v) The nominated 'Executor' should not be the beneficiary, but a trusted person – both these persons should be much younger. vi) It is not mandatory to register. vii) In addition to describing how and to whom the wealth should be distributed, including to allocation for charity, it could also convey others matters such as: a) Clarifications if needed. b) Organ donation (strongly recommended). c) Details of last rites/ceremonies etc.

Summary on money matters

- One of the top priorities for elders is safeguarding and growing their wealth, to last their lifetimes.

- Those with limited wealth should not fritter away, take undue risks or give it away – even to their Children.

- Plan for the eventuality of demise of the spouse.

RELATIONSHIPS

* *

"Good relationship is a vital factor in a person's happiness"

– Conclusion by Harvard based on 8 years of study on more than 800 persons.

RELATIONSHIP & HAPPINESS

Mr. Robert Waldinger, Director, Harvard study of adult development, in his TED talk titled 'What Brings us Happiness', shared results based on 80 years study (still ongoing), based on life of more than 800 persons, from all walks of life - workers, lawyers, doctors, a past President of USA, alcoholics, schizophrenias etc.

The essence of the study is:

- Cordial and healthy relationship with family, friends and the community is the core of happiness.

- Quality of good relationships is more important than just the quantity.

- Those who have good relationships are healthiest, even in their 80's.

- Cordial relationships enable a person to remain happy, even on days when he experiences pain. On the contrary, he who has poor relationship, his physical pain gets multiplied by emotional pain.

- Good relationships slow down ageing, while loneliness arising out of poor relationships is toxic, can even kill.

Echoing the above findings, Michael Zal, in 'Successful Retirement and Ageing – Coping With Change ', observes that bonding with spouse, children, grandchildren, and also with extended family play a very vital role as they nurture the elders and offer more joy than anything else.

Managing changes in relationships

One of the key challenges is to manage and cope with the rapid changes in the society, culture and family. Comprehending and adapting to them, without compromising one's core values, lead to enjoyable relationships. These are detailed below:

Relationship between elderly couples

It may seem ironical, but, many elderly couples need to readjust as if they are newly married! Because, during the long span of 30 to 40 years of their wedded life, significant changes would have taken place, perhaps gradually in functions such as roles & responsibilities, personality traits, behaviour, interests, social outlook and spirituality, which could have gone un noticed, due to other pre occupations, till an important event including retirement, 'empty nest syndrome' happens.

Roles and Responsibilities: Till recently, role of a husband was a provider of money, safety and security to family, while the wife used to look after husband, raise and nurture children, handle the domestic affairs, manage relationships with in laws, relatives and neighbours - family and society were largely male dominated. However, in just about a generation or so, there have been significant changes, more in urban educated families.

When young, my mother never allowed me to do any domestic work, saying it's not a man's job, which suited me, and I followed it till my retirement. But later, I had to do them grudgingly. On the contrary, I notice my son and son in law perform domestic chores willingly and with dedication.

THEN - Relationship: Wife serving husband

NOW- Relationship: Husband serving wife.

Changes in personality traits and behaviour: As mentioned earlier, over a long period, changes occur in these aspects in most people, but the extent seems to be more significant among women, particularly in assertiveness, self confidence, skill in managing relationships and decision making.

I got married forty four years ago. My wife hailed from a conservative family, brought up in a protective environment. She was shy, submissive, lacking in confidence. Over the years, she has become extroverted, assertive and self –assured. And when I look at families of my relatives, friends and other contacts, the story appears same.

Pampering: Among some elderly couples, one treats the other like a kid – giving instructions for even mundane things - what to wear; which food to eat and which one should be avoided; handing over the medicines at prescribed times etc. The result could be - one becomes totally dependent on the spouse for everything. This could pose problems later - when the one who pampers dies first, the pampered one could become helpless. In the reverse case, the one who pampers may feel loss of purpose in life.

Spirituality: This too could change over time. If the path is common for the couple, it offers them opportunities to pursue together, strengthening the bonding. If not, each needs to offer freedom to the other to follow her/his own path. If that's not the case, worse, if one criticises or forces the other, relationship would sour.

My wife has always been religious and ritualistic, but I was never so. But, we have learnt to give space and freedom to each other. For example, after my retirement, I fulfilled her dream of visiting all the holy shrines spread across India. She reciprocates by not trying to convert me to become religious.

Contrasting Attitudes: According to a study, majority of retired men are comfortable being idle (that includes watching TV and reading newspaper). On the contrary, majority of elderly women are keen to be meaningfully busy. This finding was substantiated in a TV talk show where all the elderly women said they actively support their Children, with tasks like cooking and child care, because that made them feel valued and respected. This contrasting attitude between elderly couples could be a source of strife.

Like a broken record: There is a tendency among many elders to repeatedly recall and narrate the same past incidents, mostly unpleasant ones. For the women, the topics are usually complaints about their husbands/in laws, while for the men, they are related to their bosses. For those on the receiving end (spouse, family members), that could be annoying.

Men Don't Get It: Most women have a penchant to vent out feelings that bothers them – an act that appears to offer relief. However, many husbands, instead of patiently listening, give advice or offer solutions, which irk their spouses.

I realised this quite late in my life, yet, I am unable to resist offering 'piece of my wisdom'.

—•—

Quarrel among senior couples

Quarrels among elders are not uncommon.

A friend shared that his uncle and aunt, both in late 70's, quarrel every day, on almost every issue, including who gets to watch which channel on the TV.

Fortunately, not all quarrels are to be taken seriously, according to Dr. Nancy Schlossberg, Professor at University of Maryland, who says that some couples *like* to quarrel as it keeps their adrenaline flowing; for a few, that's their marriage style!

For others, the reasons for fights are given below: (Source: "Why Elderly Couples Fight", December, 2012, The New York Times by Susan Seliger)

- Low moods; Irritability

- Stress

- Chronic illness - uncontrolled diabetes, hypertension etc.

- Pains; Aches; Hospitalisation.

- Major events – Loss; Bereavement; Retirement; Relocation,

- Over work; Exhaustion; Lack of mutual care/empathy

- Power struggle – To gain control over the other

- Too much possessiveness; Lack of 'space'/freedom

- Mismatch in sexual desire & fulfilment

Besides above, I have noticed a few other acts (behavioural), that results in quarrels. These are: teasing, insulting and disrespecting one's spouse, which gets aggravated when done in the presence of others.

What needs to be noted is that if the petty quarrels lead to frequent and offensive behaviour, then, that could be a sign of initial stages of dementia/Alzheimer's. In such cases, consultation with a Geriatrician is recommended.

Other common issues & counsellor's advice

There are several other issues that affect the relationship between elderly couples, as well as with their family members. I have given below the most common ones, extracted from a few magazines.

Legend: **Q** is query by a senior. **A** is advice by a Counsellor.

Q: My husband spends most of his time watching TV, reading newspaper. Other family members are also busy. No one talks to me or cares for my happiness.

A: Consciously create 'together time activities', like, drinking coffee, walking, watching TV etc. Also, do not depend on others for your happiness. Go out, meet others, do community service. These actions may offer more happiness than what your family could give you!

Q: Our Children are living abroad. They want us to stay with them to look after their kids. But we are tired of long travel; the weather doesn't suit us; there is no social life. However, we are afraid to say 'no', because, if we don't help them now, then, when we need their help, they might not. Is our Children's expectation fair?

A: Expectations from your Children is *not* fair. But you need to take control of your life - no one else will do. Firstly, stop thinking that if you don't help your Children, their life would collapse. They will manage anyway, like others. Secondly, share your difficulties with your Children and make them understand. Thirdly, your Children should learn to manage their lives without you.

Q: My son has gifted me a smart phone. While I don't know how to use, my 5 year old granddaughter knows. I feel ashamed.

A: Elders take longer time to learn new things. So, no need to feel ashamed. Technology plays only a small part of your life, and not the whole. Also it's enough to learn basic features that you need, and it's not necessary to become an expert.

———•●•———

'Empty Nest Syndrome'

Till about a few decades or so ago, a retiree used to live with Children. But this tradition is changing rapidly, as Children are relocating frequently, including to foreign countries for their betterment in education, job, wealth creation, quality of life etc. It is not always feasible that elderly parents move along with them. Besides, those who are financially secure, like to lead independent lives after retirement, the way they desire. The result is that larger numbers of elderly parents live away from their Children. Psychologists term this situation as 'Empty Nest Syndrome' (ENS). However, they caution that it is not a clinical disorder, but could be a stressful period for many, even if they had known about it in advance.

In ENS, one's flaws, idiosyncrasies, irritable behaviour etc., begin to get easily noticed by the spouse. It could become bad if a couple is at home, all the time. This could get worsened if any one or both have other issues related to health, money etc.

On the contrary, ENS has the potential to improve relationships and bring more joy as per an article in the Reader's Digest, June 2013, titled ' Empty Nest, New Start', in which the following experience by a couple was shared " When our only son left abroad for studies, we felt vacuum in our lives, and underwent stress. But after the initial period of struggle, followed by some hard thinking, we relocated to our native place, took care of our aged parents, set up own medical practice. We were also able to socialize more, pursue social welfare, follow our passion – all of which we were unable to do earlier since our son's education was our priority. Once we settled and were happy at the new place, our son was relieved, got over his sense of guilt of leaving us; he was also able to focus better on his studies"

The journal 'Psychology Today', offers more tips to manage ENS:

- Change the identity – From a Parent of a child to Parent of an *adult child*

- Look at positives – Children have become matured, responsible and independent, and that's what parents wish for.

- Scope to strengthen relationship between the couple.

- More time and opportunities to improve health, fitness and pursue hobbies.

"However, if a couple faces prolonged stress (due to 'ENS'), then mutual sharing could help. But if an elder is alone, writing the feelings in a diary can reduce the stress. If none of these work, then going to a counsellor is recommended", says Psychiatrist Dr.Anjali Chhabria.

Dr. Vijay Nagaswami, Psychiatrist, in 'The Fifty-50 Marriage: Return to Intimacy' advises "ENS is an opportunity to reinvent. Do things which were not feasible earlier".

True to above, a neighbour shared that since he was in the Indian Air Force, was transferred frequently, and lived alone for many years, while his wife lived in one place to ensure uninterrupted education for their two sons. Now, the couple enjoy the 'empty nest', spending time together in gardening and travelling.

My wife and I utilise(d) empty nest for:

- *Travel including pilgrimage*

- *Attending family events, including a few uninvited.*

- *Organising, participating re-unions and get together.*

- *Listening to concerts, attending discourses*

- *Playing indoor and outdoor games*

———•●•———

Separation and Divorce among elderly couples

"Every year, there is a rise in seniors seeking divorce" wrote a lawyer handling divorce cases in an English daily. He cited many reasons including infidelity, abuse and absence of care.

In an interview, a Psychiatrist shared that many elders are filing for divorce as soon as they discharge their parental responsibilities (like educating children/getting them married), to put an end to a unhappy married life.

A lady (80+) shared that her husband was abusive for many years but she tolerated for the sake of her two daughters. Once she got them married, she left her husband and started living independently supported by her daughters.

———•●•———

Relationship between Elderly Parents and their Children

"Your child is born of you, but not part of you"

– Swami Dayananda Saraswati

It is known that cordial relationship with Children is one of the key factors for happiness. The related challenges and opportunities are discussed below:

Parents feeling abandoned: This has been growing over the last two decades or so, as increasingly Children move and live abroad. This sentiment got accentuated during the Covid 19 pandemic, since the travel embargo prevented the Children to visit their parents even during the latter's sickness and hospitalisation. Worse, there were several cases when a bereaved elder had to arrange and perform the last rituals of the spouse. In such situations, those parents felt abandoned by their Children.

However, that misery could perhaps reduce if elders could understand the challenges and aspirations of the younger generation described below:

First - the increasing threat of job loss, which can happen at any time, whatever be the age due to factors like obsolescence of skills, AI (Artificial Intelligence), Automation etc.

Second - the continual increase in their aspirations to enhance the quality of life of theirs and securing future of their offspring. Of course, some might call it 'materialism'.

Third – the longer life expectancy of the next generation. Those who are 40 now, can expect to live upto 90 and above.

Fourth – there is a trend of increasing stress that affects their physical and mental health, and as a result, 61% Indians above age 45 want to retire before 50 according to a survey by HSBC.

Considering all the above factors, it has become necessary that young couples have to work, continually upgrade their skills, relocate anywhere in the world – all of which make Children living with their Parents difficult. Besides, even when the Children are keen to visit their parents during latter's illness or stay for long duration, it is not always easy for them due to their work pressures.

Once elderly parents understand these challenges being faced by their Children, then their expectations and ensuing disappointments could reduce.

Over Indulgence*: An article (www.grandparentsplus.org) reports that most grandparents spoil their grandchildren by being lenient and giving too much freedom. This is an area of frequent quarrels between them with their Children.

Love flow*: Often one hears a complaint from elderly parents "My Children don't give as much love that I gave them". But what they seem to overlook is the law on flow of love, which is :'just as water flows from high to low level, so is with love - from a parent to child; the reciprocation will not be the same. This can be realised if those who complain, recall that their love and priority, after marriage, shifted to spouse and then to their kids.

Can't say 'No'*: Often, relationship with Children suffer due to the reluctance/inability of parents to say 'no', when burdened with tasks.

Interference*: Many Children feel irritated, when their elderly parents offer 'advice', sermonise on values & morals, terming them as 'interference'. A few examples are:

- Objecting to son doing household work

- Not supporting daughter in law in her aspiration.

- Continual advice on how to bring up a child.

**Does this mean elderly parents should remain quiet, only offer services, and have no rights to share their rich experiences or wisdom? No.*

However, discretion, tact and balance are needed.

Hierarchy and Power Play: *For* centuries, Children, whatever the age, listened and obeyed their parents and other elders. Family, society and the work place were largely hierarchical. In a typical relationship between a father and his son, the former was authoritarian, the latter submissive. Similarly, between mother in law and her daughter in law, the former would try hard to hold on to her power over her son, while the latter strive to resist and take control.

However, in just over a generation, there have been significant changes. I recall relationship with my late father. I was so scared that I used to avoid seeing him. There were no small talks between us, but only cryptic instructions from him, and I used to stand and nod obediently. On the contrary, relationship with my son is one of equality; he doesn't hesitate to disagree; I often ask his advice on matters he is more knowledgeable. In the case of my wife and our daughter in law, the relationship began with respect, developed to care, and matured to affection - all mutual.

If elders become aware of such changes and adapt, the relationships could bring more joy.

Culture and Morality: For centuries Indians believed and adhered to certain moral values and cultural practices. However, the current generation, beginning with the educated urbanites exposed to the Western culture, have begun to deviate from that tradition, which include: choosing life partners by themselves often transcending caste/religion/race; opting for a live - in relationship; deciding to remain unmarried; not wanting a child etc. Reactions to these 'violation' by conservative/tradition bound elders are - shock, disgust, betrayal, helplessness etc. While some slowly reconcile, a few others go to the extent of severing their relationships with their Children.

In the above context, what the Mother (Aurobindo Ashram) observed could offer some clarity and solace: "Morality is neither absolute nor divine, but just human. Hence, it is arbitrary, changes over time, place and culture"

Guilty to be happy: Traditionally, happiness of parents is closely linked to that of their Children. So, when a misfortune strikes any of their Children (like financial insecurity, ill health, unhappy/broken marriage etc.), then the parents become not only stressed, but even feel guilty to be happy.

In such cases, Paul Jenner, Author of 'How to be Happier', offers an insight "A parent feeling sad in such situations is natural, but if it continues for long, that could be self defeating, even worsen the situation. Because, research and common sense reveal that only when a person is happy, he can support the one who needs help, spread hope and cheer".

Stress in Elderly Parents caused by Children

There are many stories on the above issue. A few are given below:

Proxy Parents: Dr.Datta, of the Tata Institute of Social Sciences (TISS), Mumbai, reports increase in cases of grandparents being forced to take more responsibilities. This also leads to parents doing less 'parenting'. She calls those Grandparents as 'Proxy Parents'.

Given below are true stories of 'proxy parents':

This is about the life of an elderly couple, living in a city abroad, separated by a few blocks – the man is living with the family of his daughter, while his wife with her son's. The 'proxy parents' get to meet each other in the evening, when they bring their grand children to play in a park. Perhaps, as 'compensation', the elders are given fully paid vacation for two weeks, every year, by their Children.

In a talk show, an elderly lady shared that she is disturbed since her granddaughter always calls her 'amma', since the kid's mother (her daughter in law), is a working woman, and hardly spends any time with her kid.

Many elders are unable to say 'no' to such burdens imposed by their Children. Common reasons are: economic dependence on Children; fear of not getting help if they fall sick; afraid of severed relationship with the grandchildren etc.

Domestic work: In a TV debate, all the elderly mothers complained that they are being exploited by their daughters and also taken for granted. Prodded by the moderator, most daughters confessed that they made use of their mothers for various reasons including to save money, being lazy etc.

When the moderator asked the elders why they tolerated, majority admitted that they wanted to be seen as 'useful' and not a burden. A few said they were compelled as they were not economically independent.

A lady (70+) was sharing about tiring domestic work, her keenness to move to a comfortable 'seniors community living' to relax. Just then, her daughter (40+) walked in, understood the discussion, and told me "Uncle, my mother enjoys household work. She loves to be busy always." Her mother kept mum.

Non Performing Asset Abroad (NPAA): With more Children moving abroad, it has become a common practice for their Parents to stay with them for long durations to support. Usually, most elderly women seem to undertake the domestic tasks willingly, but that is not so with all the elderly men. Borrowing a terminology from banking, these men are ridiculed as NPAA.

Caring or Controlling? Researcher Lucy Nicholson, in 'What Aging Parents Want From Their Kids', observes that there is a fine line between caring and controlling.

A few true stories below on that:

A man (70+) living alone, relocated to another city. His earlier house was equipped with exquisite furniture and artefacts. However, his daughter, living abroad instructed him to dispose everything, and, in the new house, to keep just four chairs. She was keen that her father should be able to walk freely, without getting injured. But her father was unhappy but helpless.

A lady (75+) living alone, was told by her son, again living abroad, that she should never cook using LPG due to fire hazard, and asked her to either buy food from outside or use an induction stove. Outside food didn't suit her, while a single stove took enormous time to cook. She was miserable but afraid to disobey her son.

The Covid 19 presented numerous instances when detailed Do's and Don'ts were given by Children, mostly living abroad, to their parents living alone in India. Though done in good faith, in some cases, the elders felt miserable.

However, there are exceptions. A woman (80+) told "I live independently, though my 3 daughters ask me to stay with them. Whenever they visit me, I tell them not to stay more than a week, because, they tend to give instructions, which destroys my self confidence"

Property care: Many are loaded with tasks of looking after properties belonging to their Children, more often by those living abroad. These include getting the house painted, letting out on rent, payment of taxes etc., which exert enormous physical and mental strain on elders.

Our son and daughter, during their relocations within India, and later while moving abroad, handled all the work by themselves. They didn't even share my mobile number with their estate agents or tenants so that we are not disturbed.

Summary - Relationships between seniors & their Children:

- ***Elderly parents need to be conscious about changes in society, culture and their implications within the family.***

- ***They have to adapt, but need not compromise on values.***

- ***Children need to be aware that expectations from elderly parents are usually only a few and simple, which are:***
  - ***Support***
  - ***Time***
  - ***Respect***
  - ***Love***

Relationship between Grand Parents & Grand Children

"Often, perfect love is experienced between grandparent and grandchild".

There is a unique and exceptional bonding between grandparents and their grand children. Nothing perhaps can match that relationship.

For example, a survey by a Tamil magazine asked kids which relationship (other than parents), is valued most. Not surprisingly, 64% voted for Grandparents.

One key reason is that Grandparents play several roles: surrogate (proxy) parent, care - giver, play - mate, friend, companion, mentor, confidant and guru. Another factor is the unconditional love, unrestricted freedom, limitless patience they offer. All of these are not usually matched by the parents, as they are usually burdened with work pressure, anxiety to 'future proof' lives of theirs as well as their kids.

Interestingly, these different roles played by Parents and Grandparents complement each other in providing comprehensive upbringing of the kids.

Insights to relationship between grandparents and grandchildren

"A grandchild does not make a woman feel old, but realisation that she is married to an old man".

Benefits of active role: According to Susan Adcox in 'Verywellfamily. com', various activities involving grand children, such as dropping and picking up from school, facilitating extracurricular activities, cooking, feeding, helping in studies, playing, telling bed time stories, putting them into sleep etc. strengthen the relationship between them. When these are carried out involving physical proximity, their bonding becomes stronger; otherwise, they can utilise the technology, like video calls, but that would have smaller impact.

According to Ms.Sonali Sharma, of HelpAge India, when grandparents play such active roles in the life of their grandchildren, there is an additional favourable side effect - it wins the elders more respect and love from their Children.

The third benefit is highlighted in an article in the Reader's Digest (August 2017) according to which those grandparents who spend time with their grandchildren live longer, are physically and mentally more active compared to those who don't.

I had a neighbour (90+), who was always busy in the kitchen. I assumed that she must be exhausted, and so advised her to relax more, to which she responded with a smile "I derive my happiness when I cook and serve variety of dishes to my grand children"

Learning Values: Studies show that kids inculcate values from parents as well as grandparents. That learning is more effective and long lasting when they notice those values, particularly respect, love and trust are practiced at home.

In a survey published in English monthly, when kids were asked what value they inculcated most from their grandparents, majority replied 'trust'. They also mentioned the reason for it, which was "I can share anything with my grandparents, but that's not so with my parents".

Safety & Security: An article in www.grandparentsplus.org, points out that grand children feel secure - physically, mentally and emotionally, in the presence of their grandparents, since they are not judged, reprimanded or criticised as much as their parents do.

Second Chance: For various reasons, many elders would have missed the opportunity to fully experience the joy of spending time, playing together and watching their kids grow. Now, they are given a second opportunity to enjoy those with their Grandchildren.

I realise not fully utilising the opportunities to watch, appreciate and engage with my children during their growing years, largely due to work pressures. However, I am making amends in enjoying every moment with my grandchildren.

Ego Buster: Since kids are oblivious about the 'glorious' past of their grandparents, (education, designation, wealth or fame), they easily puncture the ego of the elders. In that sense, they perform the role of a spiritual guru.

My granddaughter, when 6, used to play the role of a teacher, and demand that I, her student, obey her unconditionally. When I failed, she would 'punish' by locking me in the balcony, till I repented.

Advantage: Grandparents need not get stressed on 'future proofing' lives of grandchildren as that's responsibility of kid's parents.

THEN: Father to Son:

"Become an engineer or a doctor. Choice is yours".

NOW: Grandfather to Granddaughter:

"You can become an engine driver also – Choice is yours"

Esteem Booster: Likewise, kids are also unaware about failures and blunders, if any, of their Grandparents. They just reciprocate love, act as a therapist.

I read about a man who lost all his wealth during his early 60's and was discarded by his family. Then he began to visit and serve in an orphanage where he received much needed love from the kids. He was able to regain his self esteem.

Exceptions: Studies reveal that love for grandparent(s) is not automatically built in a grandchild (i.e. unlike parent). Hence, to develop a strong and healthy relationship, grand parents *need* to take the initiative and efforts to spend time and engage. This finding also answers a common query – why not all the grandparents have the same level of bonding with their grandchildren

What kids say about grandparents

- When I do anything wrong, I confess to them. They take care of the rest.

- They never say words like 'Hurry up' and 'No'.

- They don't mind repeating same story again and again and again

- They embarrass me by praising me too much in front of others

What young parents say about Grandparents

- When a Grandparent enters, discipline exits.

- I don't prefer children, only Grandchildren

Playing with grand children – a few tips

"An hour with a grandchild makes an elder feel young.

Longer than that, ageing accelerates!"

Not all grandparents know how to play, engage with kids so that both enjoy the time together. Based on my experience and watching others, I offer following tips:

- While playing, it helps that a grandparent also behaves like a kid. That requires overcoming shyness, embarrassment and inhibitions.

- Understand the difference between playing and teasing. The latter could irritate, disturb a kid.

- Energy is needed to play. When energy is low, grandparent can take short breaks, while keeping the kid engaged with activities like sketching & colouring.

- Every kid wants to win - always. So, it is better a grandparent loses – always.

- Kids too have moods, and sometimes they want to be left alone. A grand parent should be conscious of that and provide them the space and freedom

- Due to increased incidents of molestation, elderly men should be aware of 'good & bad touch' and behave appropriately.

Likely Issues between grandparents and grand children

In spite of the joy of grand parenting, there are several issues that many grandparents have to face which are described below:

Spirit willing but body wouldn't: Kids just want to play - 24 x 7. But grandparents have limitations – depleting energy, pains and aches etc.

Till my granddaughter was about 7, as soon as she wakes up, her first words would be "Come thatha, let us play". And she expected me to stop whatever I was doing, and obey her. Though I enjoyed playing with her, I used to get tired after some time.

Empty Nest- Phase 2: It refers to a grand parent's feeling of 'emptiness', sense of losing importance when a grand child grows up, becomes independent, prefer privacy, favour playing with friends, being engaged in electronic gadgets etc. Psychologists observe that in such situations, the position of a grandparent may be shifted to second or third level of importance from the viewpoint of a grandchild.

Most grand parents seem to overcome this phase of second phase by adapting to strategies outlined earlier in empty nest syndrome.

Relationships with siblings, relatives & neighbours

With the trend of elderly parents living away from their Children, relationship with siblings, cousins, other relatives and neighbours has acquired higher significance than ever before.

In addition, it is recommended that the Children living abroad consciously develop and maintain contacts and cordial relationship with those who could help their ageing parents living alone.

Relationships with friends

"When you talk, most others hear, a few listen.

But true friends listen to what was told as well as untold."

The Mayo Clinic emphasises the importance of friendships for happiness as it reduces stress, improves health and increases self worth. While that is true for everyone, for seniors, it is more so, since, true friendships are founded on trust built over decades.

Of late, many seniors have begun to enjoy reunions with friends from schools, colleges and former colleagues. Most seem to look forward to them, become nostalgic. Increasingly, spouses too join such events and forge new friendships.

However, as in all the cases, there are exceptions – a few avoid them. Reasons often conveyed are: 'I can't stand so and so'; 'I don't see any meaning in such events'; 'I can't afford' etc.

———•———

Relationship spoilers

Social media: This (e.g. What's App, Facebook etc.) is a double edged sword – when utilised judiciously, helps in maintaining relationships, if not, spoils quickly. As many elders are new to them, they commit the mistake of making flippant remarks that hurts. Studies also reveal that social media generate jealousy by promoting unfair comparisons.

Years ago when WA began to become popular, I was member of several groups. After the initial enthusiasm waned, and committing some blunders, I exited most; limited activity in the remaining, saved time and relationships.

Unmet expectations: Most persons would have given as well as received help in course of their lifetimes. However some keep harping about the support they gave, expecting lifelong loyalty. On the other hand, some who had received help tend to take that for granted, as if it's their birthright. Both are recipes to sour relationships.

Holding grudges: Many have unlimited memory to remember and recall incidents, mostly unpleasant, even those that occurred decades ago. However, there seems to be a difference between the two genders – while men seem to hold resentments related to work life, for women, it's about relationships. Whatever is the case, holding grudge is a recipe for misery.

Passing the grudges: As a fall out of the above, some pass on their grudges to their Children (like family jewellery), poisoning the young minds.

Inability to forgive: It is not uncommon that there are conflicts within families. However, some are unable to forgive and let go, not realising its adverse impact on their peace of mind.

Spoiler topics: Subjects like politics, religious beliefs and practices can lead to heated arguments, strain relationships. Hence, these may be avoided in discussions.

Summary on Relationships:

- ***Cordial relationship is crucial for happiness.***

- ***Investing time, effort, keeping expectations low, forgiveness are the essentials.***

- ***Formula for genial relationship is in a Tamil proverb "Kutram paarkin sutram illai'.***

  Meaning: "Finding faults spoil relationships"

ROMANCE, LOVE, COMPANIONSHIP, & SEX

Studies reveal that there is no age limit to enjoy Romance, Love and Sex. They can last a lifetime.

– Samantha, Psychologist, in 'Psychology Today'

ROMANCE, LOVE & COMPANIONSHIP

It is known that intense romance, passionate love cannot be sustained for long. Because, brain creates those feelings by secreting 'love' chemicals - adrenaline, testosterone, estrogen, dopamine, serotonin and oxytocin into our bodies, and these (hormones) gradually reduce with time.

This factor combined with other ageing issues, such as stress and boredom shrink love and romance over the years.

However these hurdles can be overcome, and romance and love can be renewed and sustained as detailed below:

Firstly, following the recommendations given in the chapter on 'Healthy Body and Mind' can help in revitalising romance and love. The other factors that support are: increased life expectancy; improved financial independence; better awareness; higher aspirations etc.

It was Valentine's Day. I was 66 then. I gifted a wind chime to my wife. She was surprised. On knowing about it, our Children were embarrassed; neighbours felt jealous; relatives became envious; friends were amused. But I continue gifting my wife on all special occasions.

Companionship: Till recently, remarriages between elders (single/ widower/widow) were scorned at. But attitudes are changing. Sensing it, many matrimonial organizations have sprung up to assist in meeting, dating, and marriage among elders. Some pioneers are Mr. Vasant of Tamil Nadu and Natubhai Patel of Gujarat. The latter even recommends 'Live-In' relationships to check for compatibility before deciding on marriage. Sociologist Patricia observes that willingness of elderly women to marry is a remarkable change, since it was common only among men. Gradually, the Children and the society also seem to understand that such remarriages promotes companionship and security. This fact was articulated well in the English movie 'Our Souls At Night', starring Jane Fonda and Robert Redford.

—•◆•—

Summary on Romance, Love & Companionship:

Age or status (single etc) is no bar to bring back romance, love and companionship to enrich lives and bring back happiness

—•◆•—

Sex among seniors

"Sexual purity brings strength and happiness"

- Sage Patanjali, author of Yoga Sutra

—•◆•—

Conflict with tradition & culture*:* It is common knowledge that Indians are uncomfortable talking about sex. In this scenario, any discussion about it, that too among the aged could be shocking; even viewed as inappropriate and sinful.

This can be expected, since, according to the Hindu scriptures describing the four Aasramas (stages) of life, at the third stage, 'Vanaprastha', a person is supposed to withdraw from all kinds of sensual pleasures. The fourth and final stage is 'Sanyasa', which is more stringent, and the person is expected to give up all attachments and live like a hermit.

Hence, anyone who believes in following the above path will find this chapter discomforting. That person may skip reading any further, and proceed to the next one. They can also get solace from experts who say that voluntary abstinence from sex does *no* harm.

All the others too can derive comfort from what The Mother (1878/1973, Sri Aurobindo Ashram, Pondicherry), had said in 'The sunlit path':

- Sexual impulse in humans is natural, spontaneous and legitimate.

- Sexual negation is absurd.

- Desire in sex should drop off naturally, spontaneously, without effort or struggle or conflict.

Research, Insights, Tips, Issues & Solutions

(Sources: 1. 'Placid about being Flaccid', by Dr Altaf Patel. 2. Dr.Dan Pollets, Boston University, titled 'Aging and Male Sexual Desire' .3 Indian Journal of clinical practice, August 2013, by Dr. K.K.Aggarwal & others. 4. 'Sexuality in the Elderly' by Gurvinder Kalra & others.5. 'It's Normal' by Dr.Mahindra Watsa. 6. Report in 'The National Institute on Aging', USA. 7. The Mayo Clinic report 'senior sex: Tips for older men'. 8. 'Guide to Intimate Relations' - The Reader's Digest.9. 'How to be Happier' by Paul Jenner.10. 'Use your Brain to Change your Age' by Dr Amen.11.Erection Changes After 50' by Michael Castleman)

- Sex is a fundamental driving force; an expression of romance, love, affection, admiration, loyalty, joy and growth. But, a recent study revealed that this factor is not considered while formulating the syllabus for the M.B.B.S course. As a consequence, doctors ignore this topic while treating patients.

- As the life span increases, expectations regarding improved quality of life also go up. One of them is sexual ability, which is considered essential for good quality of life. Increasingly, more seniors seek treatment for sexual difficulties than ever before. To meet that need, there are not only medicines, but also devices which are increasingly being used.

- Both men and women can enjoy sex throughout their lives.

- 63% of men age 80 to 102 continue to be sexually active.

- What is 'Normal' in sex cannot be defined. It is up to the couple to have mutual consent and decide to derive pleasure in a certain way. What is crucial is that one's act should not cause mental or physical harm to the other.

- Masturbation is natural, simple and a safe alternative. It is 'handy' when partner is not interested or when one is single.

- Tips for joyful sex life:

  - Cordial relationship between the couple

  - An open mind to get educated, get rid of false beliefs.

  - Right attitude and overcoming inhibitions.

  - Good health, fitness and hygiene

  - Adequate rest, sleep and patience.

  - Variety, playfulness and creativity (location, time, place, postures etc.)

- Abstaining from sex is *not* harmful (mentioned earlier, reinforced again)

Health benefits of safe sex

- Secretes 'happiness chemicals': Dopamine, Phenyl ethylamine and Oxytocin.

- Improves immunity

- Reduces risk of heart attack & stroke.

- Diminishes anxiety, stress.

- Pain killer.

- Anti depressant

- Motivates to do more exercise and eat better.

- Improves looks (makes skin smoother & tighter).

- Exercises the muscles.

- Helps in preventing enlargement of prostate.

- Improves life expectancy.

- A way to affirm physical functioning, self-confidence.

- For elderly women:
  - Improves hormonal balance.
  - Changes accompanying menopause are less marked

- For elderly men:
  - Even without ejaculation, man can enjoy sex.
  - Medications, including herbal and gadgets can help, but should be taken only after consultation with a doctor

*

"Sex and golf have one thing in common.

You can enjoy even if you are not good at it"

- Kevin Costner

Problems seniors face to enjoy sex

Women specific problems:

- Ageing factors and post menopause issues including:

  ○ Increase in dryness and itching in vagina.

  ○ Inadequate foreplay by the partner

Men specific problems:

- With age, testosterone levels decline, leading to following changes:

    ○ More stimulation to achieve, maintain erection and reach orgasm.

    ○ Shorter duration in orgasms.

    ○ Ejaculation has less force and less quantity.

    ○ Erectile dysfunction.

    ○ Excess consumption of Alcohol.

    ○ Smoking.

    ○ Addiction to drugs, porn films.

Problems to both the genders:

- Religious beliefs, inhibitions, misconceptions.

- Decline or difference in drive

- Illness, disability, diabetes, hypertension, arthritis, incontinence etc.

- Anxiety, stress

- Recovery from surgery/hospitalisation

- Side effects due to medications.

- Disability, poor fitness, lack of hygiene.

- Non-cordial relationship

- Fatigue/Boredom.

- Lifestyle changes – e.g. retirement, relocation, bereavement.

- Lack of interest in anything/Depression.

- Poor body image.

Frequently asked questions by seniors on sex

Dr. Mahindra Watsa, a pioneer in Sexology, Mumbai replies to questions posed by readers in a renowned English national daily. Common queries by elders and his answers are given below:

Legend: **Q** is question, followed by age and gender. **A** is the answer by Dr. Watsa.

- **Q** *by 50+ female*: My sex drive is high; I have sex with my husband about twice a week. I am also able to achieve multiple orgasms regularly. I would like to know up to what age I can enjoy sex.

  A: Congratulations as you are an example for many others. You can continue to enjoy sex as long as you desire.

- **Q** *by 75+ male:* I have stopped having sex with my wife, but having the pleasure by masturbation.

  A: Why are you selfish in getting the pleasure only for yourself? Have consideration for your wife too.

- **Q** *by 75 + male:* I am worried about my health due to reduced ejaculation.

  A: Lack of ejaculation should not interfere with your enjoyment. Nevertheless, go for regular health checkups.

- **Q** *by 80+ years male*: I used to enjoy occasional sex with my wife but after her death, I have problems in erection, semen quantity and reaching climax. Can this change be attributed to my wife's death?

  A: Your reaction to loss of your wife is personal to you, which would be different for every individual.

- **Q** *by 74 year male.* What tablet I should take since I have strong sexual desire but am not having adequate erection?

  A: Take the tablet……..for 6 weeks.

- **Q** *by 60+ male*: I experience sudden drop in my ability to have erection and maintain.

  A: Increase your foreplay. Take the tablet …..for 3 weeks.

- **Q** *by 50+ female*: I am happy in my married life. But my husband is losing interest in sex.

  A: There could be several factors including illness, mental/physical fatigue, over indulgence in food or drink, fear of failure etc. It is important to have regular sexual expression, combined with good health, right attitude which can keep sex alive well into twilight years.

- **Q** *by 65+ male*: I am frustrated because while I am keen and enthusiastic, my wife has no interest after her menopause. This frustration makes me think that I should have an affair with another woman.

  A: I would like to warn you to think of all the possible consequences.

- **Q** *by 60 year male*: I masturbate regularly, almost once every 2 to 3 days as I don't have a partner. Is my practice safe?

  A: There is nothing wrong in frequent masturbations. But indulge only when you are sexually aroused.

- **Q** *by 50+ years male*: In recent years, my wife, in late 40s has lost interest in sex although my interest is still high. What to do?

  A: I recommend you to find out the reason. Are you caring towards her? Are there any physical problems? If so, visit your doctor.

Meanwhile you may ask your wife to take this herbal capsule....for a month.

- **Q** *by 50+ male:* I am experiencing reduced urge, inadequate & very short duration of erection. I have tried many drugs but with limited success. What should I do?

  A: Do not take all those widely advertised drugs. Instead, consult your Doctor.

- **Q** *by 55 male:* I experience fall in vigour, reduced frequency in recent years. I want to increase it.

  A: The Mind demands more. But the Body has limitations.

- **Q** *by 50+ female:* I have no interest in sex at all but my husband still is.

  A: Do continue to enjoy pleasures of sex. You may take herbal capsules after consulting your doctor.

Stories on aspirations and beliefs about sex among seniors

- *A few years ago, I visited a friend (65), who had undergone a surgery. He signalled me to come near him, and murmured "I have a problem. I am not getting erection". I was shocked and also amused. Being a true friend, I assured him with a pun "These things 'hardly' matter now. Everything will be alright in due course".*

- *In many school/college reunions, after a few rounds of alcohol, the discussion among elderly men tends to find the status of sex life of others - perhaps to compare with their own, feel happy or sad, as the case may be.*

- *Once, I was visiting a factory with 500 employees, 70% of them being young women. Then, when I noticed an old and unused building, I expressed concern that it could pose safety hazard to the women. The manager reassured "No threat to women sir. All the men are old - above 50 years".*

———•———

Summary: Sex among seniors:

- ✓ **Sex offers several benefits to physical and mental health.**

- ✓ **There is no age limit to enjoy sex.**

- ✓ **Essentials to enjoy sex are: Open mind, Mutual consent, Love, Health and Hygiene**

- ✓ **If any problem is faced, seniors need not hesitate to consult physicians/experts.**

- ✓ **Voluntary abstinence from sex does no harm.**

SPIRITUALITY

. . . .

As rivers flowing to the sea discard their names and forms, so also a spiritual person gets liberated and unites with the Celestial Being.

– Mundaka Upanishad

I find God in: Feathers of a crow...Greenness of a tree... Sound of music...Verses from Scriptures... Touch of fire... Blabber of a child...In any joyful experience...

– Subramaniya Bharathiyar (1882/1921)
Tamizh Poet & Freedom fighter

UNDERSTANDING RELIGIOUS AND SPIRITUAL PATHS

Religious and spirituality paths, are often mistaken as same, but it is not so. There are significant differences, which are detailed below:

Religious beliefs, practices and path: Given below is a master list to indicate the level of religiosity of a Hindu - more ticks means higher level of religiousness.

Religiosity Check List

- Does idol worship, often to several Gods^.

- Performs daily prayers and practices various rituals.

- Devoutly visits temples and holy shrines.

- Reads, recites, learns, and listens to various scriptures.

- Trusts in horoscope, astrology, auspicious time & day.

- Applies symbols on body (e.g. holy ash/vermillion on forehead etc).

- Wears clothing as per the tradition & culture.

- Regularly participates in 'bhajans', 'satsangs'; attends discourses.

- Follows a religious Guru. Belong to a Sect/Mutt/Other such institutes

- Keen that her/his Children's marriage should happen within the same sect and community

^ A frequently asked question is: Why Hindus do idol worship? Often to numerous Gods, though the scriptures say there is only one Supreme Being?

The following answer from a publication by Sri Ramakrishna Math 'Hindu Gods and Goddesses' by Swami Harshananda, offers the answer "Faith in, and prayers to Gods have fulfilled a practical necessity in the lives of an average Hindu. Due to his limited mental and intellect faculties, he would not be able to grasp a formless, infinite Supreme Being. So, the idea of several Gods, in numerous forms were conceptualised to suit his faculties and tastes. However, ultimately, as his intellect evolves, he would be able to realise that the God is within him"

——•●•——

Spiritual Beliefs, Practices and Path: Like the check list for religiosity, one for spirituality is also developed. This is prepared based on life and teaching of eminent saints, scientists and poets, which is given first. The check lists follow later.

Basis for developing the spirituality check list:

- *Saint Thirumoolar* (8th century C.E, Saiva saint, called Naayanmaar): In poem 'Padamaadum koil'. "There are two kinds of temples. One is stationary which contains pictures of Gods. Other is moving, residing in all the living beings. When offering is made at any stationary temple, it does not reach the God. But when it is given to poor, it reaches Him.

- *Swami Dayananda Saraswati* (1824/1883, Social reformer, Founder of Arya Samaj), in 'Cultural India.Net': "Utilise your energy to improve life of all humans, without any discrimination, instead of wasting energy and time in unnccessary and empty rituals".

- **Gurudev Rabindranath Tagore** (1861/1941. Poet, Philosopher, Social reformer). In poem 'Deeno Daan', a saint told his king "There is no God in that temple you built". The king yelled "Are you an atheist? Can't you see the temple, the decorations of the God with gold and precious stones? And all the rituals are being performed?" To which, the saint replied "When your people starved and you ignored them, that's when the God left that temple you built and chose to live among the poor "

- **Swami Vivekananda** (1863/1902. Hindu monk, Philosopher, Social Reformer), In ' I am a Voice Without a Form':

  - Religion exists only in love, not in any place of worship.

  - When a man, with impure mind worships to get rid of his sins, that is useless and degradation to humanity.

  - On the contrary, anyone who serves the poor is a true Mahatma.

- **Mahatma Gandhi** (1869/1948. Indian Freedom fighter, Social reformer): "My God is Truth. Truth is my God".

- **Sri Aurobindo** (1872/1950. Philosopher, Yogi, Poet, Nationalist). "Religious life is the first step to Spiritual life".

- **The Mother** of The Aurobindo Ashram, Pondicherry (1878/1973. Spiritualist, Disciple of Sri Aurobindo) in 'The sunlit path': "The belief that God is creator means he is different from creation, which you should reject. Because of the Oneness of the divine, there is nothing but Him, in the best as well as in the worst. Religion was divine in its origin, but later became human - spreading fear and superstition. That act blocks spirituality"

- **Bhagwan Ramana Maharishi** (1879/1950, Hindu Sage). In 'Heart is Thy Name' & After the Rain': "That you are not your body and your true self is Iswara can be realised by continual self enquiry. That is the greatest service you can give to the world"

- **Albert Einstein** (1879/1955, Scientist & Philosopher): "Man believes he is separate from the rest – that is imprisonment. To enjoy freedom, he needs to be compassionate to all creatures. God and Nature are one and the same. When a man is able to realize that, he too becomes eternal"

- **Dr. S.Radhakrishnan** (1888/1975, Philosopher & Former President of India): "It is not God that is worshipped, but the authority that claims to speak in His name"

- **Jiddu Krishnamurti** (1895/1986, Philosopher, Speaker & Writer), in 'The Challenge of change'. "If God created us, then we are part of him – Omniscient, Omnipresent, full of love and joy. But in reality that is not so since we are filled with fear. To feel safe, we created God. To feel love, happiness and realise the truth, there is no need for religions, ceremonies and places of worships. Truth is like a vast open land. There is no single, correct path. Every individual should be given the freedom to find and follow his own path".

- **Baba Amte** (1914-2008, Social Reformer): "I searched Soul and God, but could not find either. But when I looked at other humans as my brothers & sisters, I discovered both Soul and the God."

- **The Dalai Lama** (1935/--, Tibetan Religious leader & Spiritualist) in 'The Art of Happiness ': "One can be spiritual without being religious. In some cases, one can manage even

better. Whether one believes in God or not, Spirituality is same –
Goodness, Kindness and Compassion".

- **R. Chudamani** (1931/2010. Tamil Writer, Spiritualist) in
story titled 'Thirumanjanam'. A young widow, showers affection
on an orphan kid, but her father, a temple priest, objects to
that relationship. One day, the father invites her to witness
'thirumanjanam' (a ritual of giving bath, followed by dressing and
floral decorations to an idol). When she questions the meaning of
such rituals, he replies "those rituals are carried out by treating
God as a human and showing affection". She then asks "Isn't the
opposite way better? Seeing and treating any human being as
God?" The father, after introspection realises the meaning of true
spirituality.

———•———

Based on the above, a check list for spirituality is developed and given
below. The number of items ticked is an indication of one's spiritual
level.

The spirituality Check List

- Believes God is within. Aspires to realise and experience it.

- Does regular meditation, contemplation and introspection. Practices
the insights acquired to progress on spirituality.

- Shows compassion to all forms of life - humans, animals & plants.

- The other qualities of a spiritualist are:

  ○ Neither believes nor practices any form of discriminations based
  on sect, caste, religion, language, race, nationality etc.

  ○ Follows rational, logical, scientific oriented thinking.

O May have a Guru/Mentor, or endeavour to discover own path.

O Atheists and Agnostics can also be Spiritualists. Some eminent persons in that category are:

- Bertrand Russell (1872/1970. FRS, Mathematician, Philosopher)

- Meghnad Saha (1893/1956. FRS. Astrophysicist, Member of Indian Parliament)

- Stephen Hawking (1942/2018, FRS, Physicist, Cosmologist).

- Vijay Tendulkar (1928/2008, Marathi Writer, Playwright, Social commentator.)

- Amartya Sen (1933/-), Economist, Philosopher, Nobel Laureate.

——•◆•——

Doubts and Clarifications: Following are common doubts raised by persons who wish to pursue spirituality. The answers are sourced from sayings of eminent spiritual leaders.

Query by a 70+ atheist: Isn't it too late for me to pursue the Spiritual path?

Answer from The Dalai Lama's book 'Art of Happiness': It is never too late for any one, including an atheist, to pursue spirituality. Because, I know many who started serious spiritual practice quite late in their lives, some even in their 80's. Yet, they were able to become highly realized Masters.

Query by a 45+ person: How do I know that I am progressing on spirituality?

Answer from Bhagwan Ramana Maharishi: When a similar doubt was raised to him by English author Paul Brunton (1898/1981), quoted in book 'A Search in Secret India', his reply was: "How do you know you have made no progress? Often, it is not easy to perceive one's progress in spiritual realm".

Query by a 60+ spiritualist: I know I am making progress. But I feel it's too slow.

Answer from The Dalai Lama: Spiritual development takes long time. Do not expect quick fix solutions. Through Buddhist training, my mind has become much calmer, but it has come gradually, perhaps centimetre by centimetre over many decades.

Steps to progress on Spiritual path

After getting inspired by the life and teachings of spiritualists, developing the check list, and finally getting doubts cleared, I have developed a methodology by which anyone can assess his level of spirituality, and make further progress.

The check list is in the form of two Tables, which are given below. The first one is preliminary, while the second is more advanced. The third is in a text form, is ultimate and follow later.

Procedure to use the table: Against each item under the Subject column (no.1), check if your behaviour fits into 'evolved' or 'not evolved'. The scores under each of them reveal your current level of spiritual development. You can progress further by sustaining the former and acting on the latter. Usually, the progress could be small, incremental and gradual as mentioned earlier.

1	2	3
Subject	**Evolved**	**Not evolved**
Converse about	Exchange ideas & Share insights.	Exchange gossip & discuss news
Listening	More	Less
Talk in	Low voice, Soft tone	Loud voice. Harsh tone
Learning	Open minded.	Close minded.
Get 'High' from	Meditation. Prayer.	Drugs. Liquor
Interests & Hobbies	Music. Nature. Books. Community service.	TV. Newspaper. Social media.
Watch talent and	Get inspired.	Become jealous
When mistakes happen	Take responsibility & learn	Avoid responsibility & blame.
While availing service	Patience.	Impatience.
In any activity	Check nuisance to others	'I don't care'
Seeking	Self awareness	Other's approval
Appreciation	Give to others	Expect from others
Faults by others	Tolerant	Intolerant
Being with self	Solitude leading to peace	Loneliness leading to depression
Play games to	Enjoy	Win
Eat when	Hungry	Bored
Choice	Nutritional. Balanced.	Spicy & fatty
Eat till stomach	Never above 80%	Always 100%

Table 1: Spirituality Assessment & Progress Monitoring – Preliminary

———•———

1	2	3
Subject	**Evolved**	**Not evolved**
Relationship basis	*'Vasudva kudumbakaham '*	*Clannish.*
Relationship reason	*Compassion.*	*Selfish motive*
Relationship nature	*Equality. Mutual love.*	*One Up (wo)manship.*
On facing problems	*Opportunity to grow*	*Hurdles to avoid*
On noticing faults in Others	*Reflect & Introspect*	*Criticise & Condemn*
Utilise wealth for	*Welfare of needy.*	*Gratification of self.*
Dominant mental state	*Peace. Equanimity*	*Aggression. Anger.*
Integrity & Honesty	*Due to concern for people & environment*	*Out of fear of punishment*
Values	*Non negotiable.*	*Negotiable.*

Table 2: Spirituality Assessment & Progress Monitoring (Secondary)

Spirituality assessment & progress monitoring - Check your score.

- **Maximum score (Primary + Secondary): 30**

- **Score under column 3 (indicator of spiritually evolving): ....**

- **Score under column 5 (indicator of spiritually yet to evolve): ....**

The Third and Ultimate level of Spirituality

This comprises of six elements, all of which, if pursued relentlessly, will lead to the ultimate level of Spirituality – a state of eternal peace and joy.

1. **Thoughts:** "Great things are born from a quiet mind", said Jiddu Krishnamurti. Watching thoughts, but without judging offers two benefits –reduces its numbers and eliminates negativity.

    Since beginning to notice my thoughts, I was surprised to notice fleeting moments of pride, jealousy, grudge etc., which I was unaware earlier – a step in spiritual progress.

2. ***Silence:*** "Silence is the speech of the Self"- Bhagwan Ramana Maharishi, which he practiced throughout his life.

    In the book "Quiet", Susan Cain points out the excessive importance given to 'extroversion', and being quiet and introverted is mistaken as inferior.

3. ***Solitude:*** *"Miseries of a man is due to his inability to remain alone"* - Blaise Pascal (1623/1662), French Scientist & Philosopher.

    Solitude is being in a state of peace even while being alone. In contrast, loneliness is feeling miserable even while being among people. It is most relevant to the aged, since many might end up being alone in their last phase of life. So practicing solitude not only enhances spirituality but also prepares them for the eventuality.

4. ***Mind Control:*** *"As is your mind, so you are. As is your breath, so is your mind. Hence, control of breath leads to control of mind"- Kriya Yoga.*

This is because, there are commonalities between the mind and breath: Both are - part of air; similar in mobility; same origin.

5. **Meditation**: *"All kinds of thoughts arise in meditation. But that's right because only when they arise, they can be destroyed" - Bhagwan Ramana Maharishi.*

    This counsel would be encouraging to those who get discouraged if they struggle to get rid of thoughts.

6. **Intellect driven:** Intellect is different from intelligence, the latter being an *external* process - gathering information and knowledge, usually from formal education. On the contrary, intellect is an *internal* process, comprising reasoning, comprehension, introspection and action. As spiritual growth takes place, influence by the mind reduces and increasingly intellect takes control.

The ultimate spirituality – Practicing the above six elements will lead to a state when a person begins to identify himself with all forms of life. This helps him to gradually shed his ego and get rid of attachments.

My Spiritual Journey

From age 6 till 16, I was in a boarding school run by a Theosophical Society in Madras (now Chennai). My school mates hailed from several religions, regions, races, cultures and economic status. Our daily morning prayer began with the recital of passages from - Quran by a Muslim boy; Bible by a Christian; Tripitaka by a Buddhist and Bhagwad Gita by a Hindu. My class mates were from families with high diversity - film stars, writers, land lords, neighbourhood 'kuppam' (slums), and refugees from Tibet. Our classes were held in thatched cottages or under the trees.

That period imbibed in me the values of non discrimination. Later I watched my father conducting Kamba Ramayana classes to villagers. He also supported higher education to the underprivileged. For instance, he helped graduation of the son of our village washerwoman, who went to the same college as my younger brother and nephew. Watching such events further strengthened my spirituality.

But, later in adult life, when I tried to 'know' God, confusion crept in. Because, God was being 'described' variously as: Nirguna' (no quality), 'Super Consciousness' etc. One extracts of Vedanta published by a reputed Hindu Mutt concluded "God is beyond understanding of human mind".

Then initial clarity came from "Vedanta – A Treatise "by Shri A. Parthasarathy (1927/--, exponent of Vedanta, Pune). Its essence: "To know God, words like 'Omniscient', Omnipresence' etc. are used, which, by themselves are not known. But, one unknown cannot be understood through another unknown. That is not logical. On the contrary, Vedanta is based on logic and reasoning with a scientific approach. Unfortunately even the educated and intelligent accept religious doctrines and dogmas without applying intellect".

I realised that to know God, I should deploy my reasoning power.

The opportunity came when I read 'How to Know God' by Dr. Deepak Chopra. Its essence incorporating my understanding is:

Any one's spiritual journey can be divided into following 7 stages – first being the beginning, and the seventh, the culmination. Each stage explains a man's understanding and his relationship with God, which is based on his fears, beliefs, aspirations, mind and intellect. These seven stages are as follows:

Stage 1: God is the Protector.

Man lives constantly under fear. His sole purpose is survival and he believes that God alone can protect him. Man aspires for the basic necessities, which are – safety, food and shelter. The man is also afraid of God, fearing punishment.

Stage 2: God is Almighty:

Once the basic needs are met, man desires for power, wealth and success. He believes those also can be given only by God, because He is Almighty and has unlimited power. So, the man, as he does with other fellow humans, does similar acts to the God also – pleads, begs, cries, praises, bargains and negotiates.

Stage 3: God is Peace:

Man is evolved, his desires have reduced. So he is more at peace with himself, shifting his focus from outward (seeking wealth & power) to inward (contentment). Thus the man has made progress in spirituality.

Stage 4: God is Love:

Man makes spiritual leap. He is full of compassion, can easily forgive anyone even those who hurt him. He begins to merge his identity with all forms of life, gradually losing his ego.

Stage 5: God is with unlimited potential.

Man realises that he has unlimited potential. Not only he is enlightened, but can enlighten others too, without the need to utter a single word, with his mere presence.

Stage 6: God is creator of miracles.

Man can perform miracles (acts which are un imaginable for ordinary men), like knowing the past, present and the future. Man utilises his miraculous powers to serve the poor, the needy, and helps every human to progress on the path to spirituality.

Stage 7 God is pure Being.

There is no more distinction between the man and God. Man has become God. He has united with Himself.

Commentary on the seven stages described above

- The seven stages are *not* 'water tight compartments', i.e., most of us would have different shades of many stages, which is logical, because, progress in spirituality is continual, gradual and unique to every person.

- On introspection, I notice myself, though for fleeting moments and in small parts in stages 3 (Man is in peace) & 4 (Man is in love). I also realise that appreciating Nature comes first and quite easily; then comes caring and loving animals, including insects – this was not difficult. However, while trying to love all humans is still a huge struggle for me, due to self righteousness, being judgemental, holding grudge etc. I have the conviction to overcome all of these stumbling blocks over several rebirths.

- That confidence arises when I recall the lives of saints of recent past, who had lived in stages 4, 5 (man is with unlimited potential), 6 (man creates miracles), and perhaps 7 (man unites with God).

  A few examples of such saints are:

  - Mahatma Gandhi, on numerous occasions, had forgiven those who harmed him.

  - Bhagwan Ramana maharishi built 'Samadhi' for cow, deer and dog, since he treated all living as equal.

- Shirdi Sai Baba performed miracles to save lives during outbreak of cholera.

- Saint Vallalar felt sad whenever he saw rice fields dying due to lack of water due to his immense compassion for all forms of life.

THEN-My Spirituality: Searching for the God, the Creator.

Summary on Spirituality:

- ✓ Being religious is the initial step to become a spiritualist.

- ✓ Spirituality is realising and experiencing that God, Truth, Love, Compassion and Nature are one and the same.

- ✓ Atheists and agnostics too can be Spiritualists.

- ✓ Spirituality is the path to experience eternal Peace and Joy.

- ✓ Every person has the potential to attain that state

RETIREMENT, HOBBIES & RELOCATION

"The Top Five Regrets of the Dying"

- Bronnie Ware's findings

1. *Instead of being true to myself, I lived to impress everyone.*

2. *I didn't spend enough time with my family.*

3. *I didn't express my love to family & friends.*

4. *I failed to build and nurture relationships.*

5. *I prioritised on wealth instead of happiness.*

———◆———

Good News: *Any or all of the above mistakes can be corrected by anyone at any time.*

It is never too late

OPPORTUNITIES AND CHALLENGES AFTER RETIREMENT

There are plenty of opportunities to enjoy life after retirement, but there are a few challenges too. If these can be understood and acted upon, life could be happier than ever before.

Firstly there have been huge changes in the lives of seniors compared to earlier generations, which are summarised in the table below.

Factors	SENIORS THEN	SENIORS NOW
Life expectancy	Around 55.	85. Will continue to increase.
Retirement Age	Around 60	Increasing early retirements.
Financial security	Mostly dependent on Children.	Increasing less dependency on Children
Living	With Children, Siblings etc.	Decreasing trend of living with Children.
Place to settle down	Home town / Ancestral village	Many don't have a functional 'home town'.
Life style	Contented. Mundane.	Many aspirations. Self actualisation.
Support & Help from	Children, siblings& relatives	Increasing dependence on paid services.
Travel	Limited to holy shrines.	Visiting children, leisure & sightseeing.
Entertainment	Limited to family events, festivals.	Larger, widened scope.
Relationship with Children	Patriarchal. Hierarchical	Increasing delegation of authority

When should an elder retire?

This depends on several factors which are outlined below:

Monetary Security: The key factor to decide is the financial security. The answer could be obtained from the earlier chapter on 'Money Matters'.

Retirement age vs. Longevity *(Source: 'Optimum Strategies for Creativity and Longevity', by Sing Lin, USA, March 2002).*

- Average life expectancy for 'late retirees' (age 65 and above), is 67. Probable reason is high stress causing long-term serious health problems.

- On the contrary, average life expectancy of 'early retirees' (age 55) is much higher at 86. Probable reasons could be better advanced planning, higher wealth, limited aspirations etc., which enabled them to retire early.

- However, the early retirees did not idle, but continue to be active, including doing part time or full time work, pursuing other interests, community service etc., which do not cause undue stress.

On similar lines, Dr. Deepak Chopra, refers to 'Early Retirement Death', highlighting the increased incidences of heart attacks and incidences of cancer in the first few years after retirement, which are attributed to a common feeling among retired men that their useful days are over.

Opportunities after retirement

Most working persons eagerly look forward to the retirement. Some do so even from age 40 onwards to lead a life of leisure and relaxation, to enjoy the fruits of hard work, pursue various interests that couldn't be done earlier.

Given below are the various factors that offer opportunities to increase happiness after retirement.

Increased life span: As mentioned earlier, the living period after retirement is increasing steadily, and will continue to do so. Assuming one retires at 60, and goes on to live till 85 or even more, that is 25 + years – a long period offering enormous opportunities.

Stronger relationships: With no work pressure, and plenty of leisure time, this period could be the best phase to (re) build, strengthen relationships – with spouse, children, grandchildren, relatives and friends. For those who have been 'workaholics', they get a second chance.

Besides, with plenty of time available, seniors can also forge new relationships – this is also desirable since friendships with former colleagues and neighbours could fade away over time.

Improved financial security: Increasingly more elders are in a better financial status than ever before. They have opportunity to fulfil their 'bucket list'.

Opportunity to re-invent: These are activities that one does for the first time in life, which are feasible if one is open minded and not afraid of failures.

After retirement, we moved to an apartment in a newly built condominium in Bangalore. I formed the owners' association, coordinated with the builder and ensured all the amenities were made operational. I headed the association for five years, mentored the youngsters, and handed over the management to them.

I wrote and published my first book, titled "Arranged Marriage – Guide for finalising compatible alliance".

Improving Health & Fitness: This may sound strange but as already elaborated, even if one had ignored his health & fitness, amends can be made to improve them and enjoy better quality of life.

Health and fitness of my wife and mine have improved after turning 60.

Travel etc.: More than ever in the past, seniors now undertake travel. Some even go for trekking, a few venture on cross country cycling, adventure sports etc.

My wife and I have travelled most after retirement, not only to holy shrines but also holiday destinations besides visiting and staying with Children abroad.

Work after Retirement: There are many who opt to continue to work for varied reasons. Types of work could be: full or part time; remunerative or non- remunerative.

Paid work could be taken to: increase pension corpus; pay liabilities - own or Children; for future major contingencies; enjoy luxuries like vacation abroad; gift to family members; charity etc.

Un paid work, full or part time is usually taken up to remain active; contribute to society; for passion.

———•———

Challenges after retirement and overcoming them

Yes, the much awaited life after retirement could pose many challenges too - emotional, behavioural, sociological, health, financial etc., leading to stress, anxiety and unhappiness if these are not managed well. These are identified and possible solutions are provided below.

Work after retirement: The retiree need to have clarity on why he would like to *work*. He also needs to foresee potential stressors, health hazards, preferably discuss with spouse/Children, and then make the commitment.

A popular choice is continuing to work in the same organization - full or part time; same or different function/location. This option offers several advantages: continuity and comfort. But there are pitfalls too - the retiree might feel disappointed, even bitterness, if he perceives a lowered status.

Boredom: Decades ago, Philosopher Bertrand Russell, wrote in 'Conquest of Happiness' "Several of my retired friends and acquaintances have expressed their problem of getting bored and their problem of not knowing what to do".

This observation is relevant even today for many who don't have any hobbies or interests. However, anyone can identify and develop new interests and hobbies at any age, which is dealt with later.

Loss of self esteem: In "Man's Search For Meaning", Viktor Frankl observes that many who cease to be busy feel lack of meaning in their lives. Some could even sense a void within them.

This is true for those who had identified their values with their profession, positions, power and perquisites. The sudden loss of these could result in lowered self esteem.

To overcome these issues, Michael Zal in "Successful Retirement and Ageing... ', and counsellor Elizabeth Holtzman, in "Emotional Aspects of Retirement' suggest that one can realise that there is more to life than one's job/profession by widening their identity and role. This could be as a: supportive spouse; active grandparent; responsible citizen; social activist etc.

Resentment & Disappointment: It is likely that some retirees carry this negativity long after retirement. Psychologist Erik Erickson terms it as 'Low Emotional Integrity (LEI)'.

I was chatting up with a retired colleague, who recalled an incident that occurred thirty years ago and began to abuse his boss. It was evident that he has not been able overcome his resentment.

Inability to relax: Poet Mary Oliver said "Idle and be blessed". In Psychology Today, Jeffrey Davis quotes research findings that human brain is wired for laziness. However, some instead of enjoying a relaxed life, continue to live a hectic life and get stressed, perhaps due to advice most receive since childhood that one should be always busy. Perhaps, they feel guilty for not doing anything.

In a national daily, a person narrated the following incident "My close friend has been leading a stressful life, was looking forward to retire and relax after 60. However, soon after retirement, he announced a new venture. I advised him not to, since he was looking forward to a life of leisure where as what he plans to do will be more stressful than ever. On listening to my counsel, he became angry, accused me of being jealous. I realised that some of those who have been leading a hectic life cannot relax".

After my retirement, whenever anyone asked me what I am doing, I felt uncomfortable to say 'nothing'. However, when I spoke to a former colleague, his response was "I am happy doing nothing. I have worked hard all through my life. Now, I am enjoying the fruits of that effort. I deserve it". That gave me clarity.

Disillusionment: Many have dreams of how they would like to spend the years after retirement and when this fails to happen, disillusionment arises.

A man (75+) shared "I was passionate about tree plantation, which I pursued after retirement. I was happy. However, after turning 70, my health didn't permit that activity. I feel a void in my life…"

Irritability: There are many who had enjoyed enormous power and perquisites during work life, could feel handicapped on losing them after retirement, leading to irritability. This feeling is often passed on to spouse and other family members.

In a workshop for retirees, the counsellor suggested that a retired man should move out of the house, for a few hours in the mornings and also in the evenings, preferably to do community service. Besides, while at home, he should share the work load with spouse.

The wife too has a role to play by tactfully involving the husband in house hold chores, appreciating him, and continuing to give the same level of respect (?!) as before.

Visits to holy shrines: Many elderly women have complained that their husbands don't escort them to the holy shrines. But the husbands have their reasons, such as: "I am not religious"; "Places of worships have become commercialised"; "We will go some time later" etc. In support of the women, I have following reasoning based on my experience: Any place where large numbers pray together spread positivity, including to those who are not religious. Secondly, travel by itself brings joy. And most importantly, such travels strengthen the bonding between the couple.

Challenges in Voluntary Work: This may surprise some, but even good intentioned voluntary work could pose hurdles, even create stress.

Couple of years ago, a few of us visited a village school to assess their needs and offer help. During the discussion with the Headmistress, we understood that the school is short of teaching staff, and so we offered our services. In another instance, a retired professor told that he went to a government college near his house and volunteered to teach, free of cost. In both the above instances, the offer was not taken. On investigation, it was found that the existing staff felt insecure by 'outsiders'.

An acquaintance told "After retirement, for the last ten years, I have been doing voluntary work in a reputed, pan - India spiritual organisation. Initially I was disappointed when I noticed conflicts among the 'Swamis' who manage it. But soon I learnt to stay away from the politics and continue my contribution"

A retired teacher shared that her voluntary work for physically challenged children does not allow her to take leave when needed, since that disturbs the schedule of the students. This, she said, often caused distress to her as well as her husband.

Tips to overcome post retirement problems: *(Source: Darrel Sifford in 'Mining The pleasures for a happy retired life')*

- *Plan:* At least five years ahead of retirement, begin preparations.

- *Purpose:* As you wake up in the morning, look forward to some work that's non- stressful, stimulating and for the welfare of the community.

- *Learn:* Continue. Make it a habit.

- *Share:* Teach, coach, mentor the under privileged.

- *Optimism:* Look at the future with hope and enthusiasm.

- *Reinvent:* When not sure, try different things. You will find one that gives joy.

Interests, hobbies, passion, becoming a connoisseur

"Life becomes a paradise for anyone who loves many things with a passion" said Leo Buscaglia, Professor, and University of Southern California.

A recap on the meaning and differences between related terminologies:

- *Interest*: Is a *feeling*, curiosity or desire to know or learn about something.

- *Hobby*: Is a regular *activity*, for joy, and relaxation, but not for money.

- *Passion*: Is when a hobby is pursued with love and dedication.

- *Obsession*: Is when passion becomes a fixation.

- *Connoisseur*: Is a person whose passion and obsession are combined with extra ordinary knowledge and talent.

The Good News: Paul Jenner, in 'How to be Happier' observes "Many have a dormant gene, which can be awakened with exposure to varied experiences. This could lead to a hobby, even a passion"

I never had any interest in Carnatic music till my retirement, but developed interest, which later became a passion.

THEN: Dormant interest in music

NOW: Awakened interest, became a passion in music.

Summary on life after retirement – work, interests and hobbies:

- ✓ *Advance planning prior to retirement helps.*

- ✓ *This phase offers opportunities to realise unfulfilled wishes.*

- ✓ *But there are challenges too, which can be managed.*

- ✓ *It is never too late to identify and enjoy new hobbies.*

RELOCATION

"Due to significant changes in culture, society and aspirations, home is no longer the place of birth or where one grew up.

Instead, it's the place that offers peace."

– Adapted from quote by Nobel Laureate Naguib Mahfouz

As the retirement date approaches, an important but often a difficult question arises for many– where to 'settle down permanently'?

As pointed out earlier, about 40 years ago, this question would not have arisen for many, since they would live with their Children or remain/relocate to home town. But, among this generation of elders, many had migrated to other parts of the country. Now, their Children have gone a step farther, becoming globe trotters.

Hence, for many, relocation after retirement offers challenges as well as opportunities.

The various options, followed by factors that help to make the decision are given below:

1. Options to relocate and live:

    a) With Children

    b) Near to Children

    c) Close to siblings/relatives/friends

    d) At home town

    e) None of the above.

        i. Stay at the same place (no relocation).

        ii. Move to a Seniors Community Living (SCL)

2. Factors that need considerations before finalising any of the above option:

    • Safety

    • Security

    • Medical services

    • Cost & Affordability (till end of life of both)

    • Spirituality (avenues to pursue)

    • Camaraderie (companionship).

    • Opportunities for entertainment, hobbies etc.

    • Ease of connectivity to essential destination by – Air, Rail, Road

    • Pollution free environment (Air, Noise, Water)

    • Compatible weather

Additional details to help decide on relocation

Live with/nearby Children: This option could perhaps be the preferred option for many. However, issues could be: possible burden of full time care of grand children ('proxy parents') leaving little time for other pursuits. If elders relocate to a foreign country to live with Children, additional difficulties could be: lack of avenues for entertainment, constraints to travel independently, limitation to pursue spirituality; inclement weather etc.

Live close to Siblings/Relatives/Friends: This is often the next best option, provided the relationships are cordial. On the contrary, some prefer to stay away from their relatives.

Return to home town: This is usually attractive due to sentiments and reconnecting with relatives and friends. But, check list points to be verified.

No relocation: This saves lot of hassles, and a good option if the important factors are taken care of. However, some stay put in the same place in spite of several disadvantages (of the present location), for which reasons could be - strong emotional attachment (to the house, neighbourhood); lethargy; indecisiveness; no consensus between a couple/with Children (details later).

Moving to a Seniors Community Living (SCL): *Details in next chapter.*

True stories of relocation

Children on the move: Many relocate to live with or in close proximity to their Children, ignoring the fact that many youngsters are on the move.

After retirement, my wife and I relocated from Pune to Bangalore, because our son was living there, and our daughter was planning to join us. However, within six years, both moved abroad. We realised that in these days, we can't expect our Children to stay put in one location.

Dream vs. Reality: *A friend relocated to another city because a few of his college mates lived there and hence expected to relive those 'good old' days. To his dismay he found the nature of relationship had changed; besides he didn't take into account that spouses of the friends also need to get along. Two years later, he returned to place where he moved from.*

Another bought an orchard at his ancestral village with lots of dreams. But in less than three years, he lost much of his pension corpus. He moved to another city to live in a rented premise.

No consensus: In several instances, there are serious differences between the couple on where or when to relocate.

In one case, a senior wanted to remain in India to support his ailing mother, while his wife wanted to migrate to USA as her siblings have settled there. The issue became so serious that they were even contemplating divorce.

Logistics nightmare: Many who desired to relocate are unable to do so as the logistics of relocation are intimidating. Often their Children, particularly those living abroad are unable to spend much time and effort to help in relocation. Eventually they reconcile to continue to live in the same place, though unwillingly.

Status Quo: There are also instances where retirees, whose Children live abroad continue to stay in the same place, in spite of it being far away from their home town and relatives. A major factor is their cordial relationships in the community, cutting across language and cultural barriers. A few do so to remain away from relatives!

Role of Children: Often, Children, particularly those living abroad, decide where, when and if at all their elderly parents should relocate. In such cases, it is vital that the Children understand the aspirations and challenges of the aged. One specific area of frequent disagreement is related to moving to live in a Seniors Community Living, which is detailed later.

<hr>

Summary on life after retirement -Relocation:

- ✓ *Leo Tolstoy said "When I relocated from my village to a city, my anguish was like uprooting a hundred year old oak tree" - true for many seniors even now.*

- ✓ *Any relocation is complex and stressful. But can be done. We did three times after retirement.*

- ✓ *Taking decision early is crucial as relocation would become increasingly difficult as years pass by.*

SENIORS COMMUNITY LIVING (SCL)

"Why can't I too, retire from work, like you?

When can I also lead a life of leisure and pursue my interests?"

Radha (my wife) to me, five years ago

"SCL has offered me the life I aspired for."

Radha to me, now.

SENIORS COMMUNITY LIVING

Seniors Community Living (SCL) is NOT an Old Age Home (OAH): This is the first thing that many, including elders and their Children need to understand, since, there is lot of mis understanding and confusion. This is detailed further.

Till about three decades or so ago, only OAH existed, which were meant for destitute. The living conditions, particularly the accommodation, food, hygiene, safety, security, medical assistance, amenities, opportunities for recreation and entertainment etc. were either poor or non-existent. The OAH's were funded and run by the State/Central Governments, NGO's/charitable institutions.

In total contrast, the SCL's are built and managed as commercial (profit making) enterprises. The living conditions and amenities vary from decent to luxurious, depending upon a senior's ability to pay.

Opportunities in SCL for Joyful living

Happy – Happy Situation: In a webinar, *a* CEO of an organization that has built SCL's across India gave following explanation on why SCL has become a fast growing business segment: "Till about thirty years ago, Indians were not culturally, socially, emotionally, financially ready for SCL. Till then, elders lived in extended/joint family structure, mostly anchored in one place, i.e., less relocation. However, thanks to globalisation, youngsters began to migrate to foreign shores for higher education, job, career and wealth building. Since elders can't cope with such relocations, the SCL gave them the solution to lead a safe, secure and comfortable environment – truly a 'Happy-Happy 'situation for both the seniors and their Children.

Women demand retirement: This is another major and a relatively new factor for SCL's popularity. Women have begun to assert, demand to retire and relax – which was never the case in the past.

I have spoken to numerous elders and realised majority of them moved to SCL, due to 'push' from the women. So is the case with me as mentioned earlier.

Medical emergencies: Most SCL have either in- house or on-call paramedical staff, ambulance, regular doctor visits etc. In addition, for the very sick, most SCL's assist in getting immediate admission to hospitals; some even have a tie up.

In the SCL where we live, I have witnessed many emergencies when the first aid was carried out within 15 minutes, and ambulance was put into service in less than 30 minutes. Availability of this kind of prompt service would be unlikely in the 'outside world' particularly when seniors live away from their Children.

Improved quality of life: Besides escaping from routine domestic work, SCL offers opportunities for camaraderie with likeminded people; indulge in variety of activities. Examples: organizing and participating in festivals; enjoying various entertainments; playing indoor and outdoor games; opportunities to display & nurture talents; go on group travels etc.

Money matters: Cost of living in a SCL, whether an outright purchase of a dwelling or under rental/lease, varies widely, and so, anyone can choose depending upon preference and affordability. Often, for those who can't afford, their Children, who are financially well off, do the funding willingly, in view of the several advantages enlisted earlier.

Higher self esteem: SCL facilitates seniors to live independently, not relying on their Children for entertainment, travel, hobbies etc. This life also offers privacy and promotes cordial relationships, all of which enhance their self esteem.

Intellectual wellbeing: Most SCL's have significant population comprising of educated professionals retired from varied fields, who have lived in many regions and countries, got exposures to variety of cultures and experiences. Interactions with such rich minds can enhance intellectual well being.

Seniors with challenged Children: Seniors with Children who are mentally/physically challenged find SCL a better option due to superior safety and security. By relieving them from many domestic chores, they get more time to interact. Majority in the community also seem to be supportive and empathetic.

A mother of a mentally and physically challenged teenager shared that for the first time in many years, her daughter was smiling more and happier after coming to live in a SCL.

Moving with family/friends: Some seniors move to a SCL, along with their parents/siblings/In Laws/close friends. In such cases, the feeling of being 'uprooted from own home/familiar place to live among strangers' is far less.

A lady in early 90's said "I am having the best time of my life. I am living in a furnished apartment with a TV - all to myself. I get food delivered to me. My two daughters and their husbands, who gifted these to me, are my neighbours.

Flexi living: For senior couples who have to look after their parent(s), often in 90's, one of them stays back in SCL, while the other goes abroad to be with their Children/Grand children. This becomes possible since food, security etc. are taken care of.

Best of both the worlds: Some wealthy people keep SCL as a second option to serve as a break from monotony. Once in a while, their Children/Grand children also come and stay in the SCL.

If elders don't want to live only among the aged, they can opt for a SCL which forms part of a large Condominium/Township, to socialise with youngsters.

Fully Assisted Living: This refers to those who need assistance for helping to do even routine tasks. Some SCL admit them along with others who don't need any such assistance, while there are dedicated ones for fully assisted living with trained professionals taking full time care. But the latter are more expensive.

Adding life to years: With a positive and open mind, if a senior chooses an appropriate SCL, he can add life to years.

———•◆•———

Young woman to husband on a visit to a SCL:
"How quickly you can turn 60?"

Challenges & Apprehensions to living in a SCL

Yes, in spite of the several benefits and advantages enlisted earlier about SCL, there are many challenges and apprehensions too, which are detailed below:

Clarity: Basic queries like why, where, when and what for one would like to move to a SCL should be answered to ensure there are no regrets later.

One chose a SCL because it had Billiards, which was his passion during his younger days. He regretted his decision as it was based on misplaced priority, since he didn't like the food and the place lacked adequate medical services.

Pain of relocation: As mentioned earlier, even in cases where Children have settled abroad, and settling down with them is ruled out, leaving one's home/place where one has lived for decades to shift to a SCL can be agonizing.

During a reunion, a friend, whose Children have settled abroad told "I can never imagine moving away from my home, neighbours and friends and the community I lived for 40 years to live in an unknown place, among strangers. I will never do it."

However, my wife and I were able to move to a SCL without much pain and we attribute that to the following two reasons: firstly, our Children had moved abroad, and they felt relieved after we explained the benefits of living in a SCL that we chose. Secondly, over the last fifty years, we have relocated twenty times, and so, we had not developed any strong affinity to any place or people.

Feeling of guilt: Some, mostly women have expressed guilt to leave their Children/Grandchildren to live in a SCL and enjoy a relaxed life. That is perhaps due to the tradition when women, irrespective of age, were expected to serve their families till their last days. It seems this has not changed much. They are put under pressure, directly/indirectly. To overcome that cultural mind set, relax and enjoy is not easy for them.

When I visited my friend (45), I was served tea by an elderly woman. My friend introduced her as his mother (70+) and then proudly showed a coffee mug which was printed with 'Everyone retires, but my mother will never'. I also learnt she was looking after her two grandchildren.

Vanvaas/End of active life?: There is a misconception among many that when a person moves to a SCL ("Old Age Home" as they often term it), that means discarding active social life and becoming a recluse. This is wrong because if one chooses the appropriate SCL, quality of life could be better than before.

Money matters*:* As mentioned earlier, SCL's have wide variations in capital and living expenses, which keep increasing due to inflation, while returns on investments in low risk options such as fixed deposits keep reducing. If these factors are not considered before moving into one, periodic increase in cost of living could become stressful.

Support during medical emergencies*:* Some are afraid to move to SCL, since they don't know who would help in case of medical emergencies. This is understandable if they already enjoy the support from their Children/Relatives. If that is not the case (e.g. Children abroad, no support from relatives), then, a well equipped SCL could even be a better option as explained earlier.

Fear & Apprehensions: Fear is largely due to the many unknowns – staying in a new place; living among strangers; suitability of the food; quality of services; favorability of the weather; reliability of medical services etc. These can be addressed by conducting proper assessment (tips given later).

Some have expressed a few specific apprehensions –one is lack of diversity, i.e., all being elders, often belonging to same community and culture.

The other is the difficulty to forge new and strong friendships at 60+. Although I noticed that those who are extroverted are able to forge new and strong bonding within a short time, others (perhaps the majority) find it hard. Some have complained of loneliness; a few showed symptoms of depression.

Cultural, Intellectual & Spiritual Fit: Cultural fit is about being comfortable with the food habits, language, dress, customs & traditions which are essential to make one feel at ease and settled. Intellectual and spiritual fit is about compatibility in education, profession, lifestyle and interests which facilitate building healthy relationships. Not taking these into consideration before moving would make one unhappy.

A man (80+) hailing from West Bengal moved to a SCL in a southern district of Tamil Nadu. He was a mis fit in every aspect. He returned to his roots, but only after undergoing financial, physical and mental strain.

Logistics nightmare: *As observed earlier, any relocation is complex and stressful. It is not uncommon that seniors have to do all or most of the work themselves, particularly when Children live abroad. Hence, many who are keen to relocate to a SCL but are unable to do so.*

Disturbing environment: *Some aspects of living in a SCL could be* disturbing compared to 'outside world'. A few examples: one would come across much larger number of persons with disabilities; listen often about serious illnesses; come to know frequently about death etc.

When we moved to a SCL, both my wife and I felt uneasiness due to the above factors. Fortunately, without much conscious efforts, our discomfort significantly reduced in about three months. Yes, it does creeps up once a while.

Besides, it is a mis conception that all the youngsters are always cheerful, where as the aged are grumpy, because age has little to do with those feelings.

Harmonious living: It's not uncommon to come across factionalism, prejudices and one-upmanship in some SCL's which could ruin harmonious living. Prevalence of any such issues should be checked before choosing one.

———•◆•———

A Recap and check list to finalise a SCL

If one decides to move to a SCL, then the following can facilitate in selecting a suitable one.

➤ *Money Matters:*

- Affordability, including increase in cost over long term (mentioned earlier)

- Type of dwelling - apartment/villa; size; layout.

- What is the reputation of the management? Are they long term players? Financially stable?

- Options: Purchase (own funding or from Children)/Long term lease/Rental.

- Scope for appreciation (of the property if one decides to sell or pass ownership to the Children after the demise of both)

- Feasibility of sale to others/ownership transfer to Children after demise of both/buy back from builder/others

➤ **Medical Services – Availability : In house/Ease of hired services:**

- Clinic & Pharmacy

- 24 x 7 paramedical staff/ambulance.

- General Physician/Specialists, close by.

- Maintenance of medical records, regular checking of hypertension, sugar levels etc.

- Reputed multi speciality hospitals in proximity.

- Tie up with hospitals for quick & prompt admission

> **Safety:**

- Panic buttons to alert Security/Medical staff. ELCB. Entrance door not self locking and with one set key with security for emergencies; Fire alarms; Smoke detectors; LPG leak detector; Fire fighting provisions.

> **Food& Beverages:**

- Freshly cooked, tasty, balanced, variety, suiting one's palate.

- Efficient, courteous service. Timings. Door delivery options.

- Common dining with fixed menu/A La Carte with choices in cuisines

- Proximity to : Food courts/Restaurants/Cafeteria/Multiplex/Bar

- Menu- Do the residents have a role in the selection?

- Is cooking at home allowed if one desires?

- Charges and related rules & Regulations.

> **Essential services:**

- 24 x 7 availability of: Security with CCTV cameras; Power/DG back up for lights, lifts (common areas) and inside residence; potable water; intercom.

- Satellite dish for TV, Broadband connection

- Sewage treatment.

- Quality of housekeeping services at residence and common areas.

- Scope of maintenance inside residence - Electrical, Plumbing, Carpentry, Civil work

➢ *Other Services – Inside or in close proximity:*

- Place of worship

- Departmental Stores; ATM. Concierge services (Banking, Travel booking etc.)

- Shuttle services/Cabs/public transport to city centre

➢ **Senior friendly amenities:**

- Wheel chair access to all areas. Anti skid tiles, grab bars in bath & toilets. Hand rails in all corridors, passages. Arthritis friendly door knobs. All bath/toilet rooms with wide doors for wheel chair access, and doors open outward. No trip hazards in any areas. Shuttle service within the premises. Adequate lighting at all locations.

➢ **Facilities for various activities:**

- Adequate open space with greenery, dedicated walking paths.

- Club house. Gym. Guest house. Library. Salon. Spa.

- Indoor & outdoor games.

- Recreation hall for get together/social events.

- Swimming pool.

- Movie theatre

➢ **Management of SCL:**

- Competent? Professional? Ethical?

- Do they facilitate forming and functioning of association of residents?

- Accessible for escalating unresolved serious issues?

- Effectiveness of grievance handling mechanism.

> **Weather:** Suitability.

> **Pollution**: Noise, Air, Water etc.

> **Neighbourhood (immediate vicinity)**: Conducive & peaceful

> **Residents' feedback:**

- What do they say? Talk to as many residents as possible.

- Observe the residents – do they appear cheerful?

> ***Stay/Live and Verify:*** Most SCL's have a guest house. It is recommended that one stay there, check mental & physical comfort levels before taking a decision. If one intends to buy, then it may be even wiser to live for a year or so, on rental and then decide.

Summary on Seniors Community Living (SCL):

Opportunities:

✓ *A suitable option, particularly if Children live abroad or those who don't have any offspring.*

✓ *Safety, security and comfortable living*

✓ *Freedom from cooking*

✓ *Plenty of choices to socialize and pursue hobbies.*

Challenges:

✓ *Social stigma of 'Old Age Home'*

✓ *Fear of many unknowns - getting uprooted from familiar place among known people to an unfamiliar place among strangers*

MANAGING PAIN & SUFFERING, ILLNESS & HOSPITALISATION, RECOVERY/FINAL STAGE

"A deep distress has humanised my soul"

– William Wordsworth

PAIN AND ITS IMMENSE VALUE!

As mentioned earlier, research has shown that intelligence resides not only in our minds, but in every cell of our bodies too, acquired since evolution.

Understanding pain: When pain is sensed, the body's intelligence takes prompt corrective actions such as through reflex, activating defence mechanism like making the blood to clot etc. Besides, body also communicates hidden illness through pain or other symptoms, signalling to mind to act. But, in contrast to the body, often the mind does not act as promptly, due to fear leading to denial mode. A physician shared that many elders are afraid of visiting a doctor even after noticing various symptoms, such as inflammation, lump, pain etc.

A woman (55+), confined to a wheel chair shared: "I recognised repeated symptoms of stroke, but I chose to ignore them; I also did not inform my family members about it. Yes, I was in denial mode. If I had acted promptly, I would be leading a normal life now".

In 'Pain, The Gift nobody wants', Dr Paul Brand, surgeon, offers insights about the value of pain. He, during his work on leprosy patients in Chengalpattu, Tamil Nadu, noticed that many were losing parts of toes and fingers. His investigation revealed that while the patients were sleeping in a dormitory and rats were chewing off their body parts, they were unaware, since they had lost the sense of pain – a side effect to leprosy. And that explains the value of pain.

Pain and its causes: *(Sources: 'Anatomy of an Illness.....' by Norman Cousins & Rene Dubos. WebMD.Com).*

Most common causes of pain are listed below. For elders, it can be from unexpected sources and hence difficult to diagnose.

- Stress, Anxiety, Tension, Worry, Suppressed rage

- Idleness, Boredom.

- Inadequate sleep.

- Over eating/Empty stomach/Poor diet.

- Inadequate exercise/Poor fitness.

- Excessive smoking/alcohol consumption.

- Poor quality air/weather, chilly winds etc.

- Wrong postures – e.g. while sitting, walking, standing, watching TV, reading, using mobile/laptop, driving, sleeping

- Incorrect way of lifting - things, grandchild.

- Foot wear- wrong size/design/worn out.

- Allergy (food/environment etc).

- Over exertion.

- Eye strain due to changed vision, over exertion.

Beware: While experiencing pain, it is vital that elders should not rush to consume pain killers as they are vulnerable for serious side effects (more details later). Easiest and first thing to do is to check if the pain is due to any of the common causes as listed above.

If not, then following points offers guidance as to when a senior should visit a physician:

- When any pain prolongs, occurs repeatedly (chronic).

- After any fall, even if there is no obvious sign of injury or pain.

- Pain in chest, left shoulder, left upper back.

- Severe headache.

- Prolonged stiff neck.

- Pain accompanied by numbness in any part of body.

- Abdominal pain combined with fever/vomiting/nausea.

Non Conventional Pain Relieving Techniques

Music as pain relief: As per "Musicophilia – Tales of Music and the Brain" by Dr.Oliver Sacks, Neurologist, music is a medicine, and it is integral to being human.

'Alive Inside', a documentary film (2014) and AARP Bulletin (2015) lists several case studies of patients suffering from Alzheimer's/Dementia had their mood lifted, felt energetic and felt less pain after listening to music.

In "Anatomy of an Illness", Norman Cousins narrates his meeting with Pablo Casals, (90), who was finding difficulty in walking and breathing, but as soon as he began to play piano, he developed enormous energy, and thereafter, he walked straight, breathed normally. He summarises "It was evident that music was his medicine. I witnessed a miracle.... "

On the same lines, Prof. Saraswathi from Sri Padmavati Vidyalaya, Andhra Pradesh, presented a research paper in Rome about pain relieving capabilities of specific ragas of classical music (e.g. Ananda Bhairavi), which she authenticated using functional Magnetic Resonance Imaging (fMRI).

A senior (75+), after a head injury and during hospitalisation, behaved aggressively, even trying to pull the tubes and cables, but calmed down when Carnatic music was played.

Reading aloud: An article 'Words of wellness' in the Reader's Digest (October 2021), narrates case studies of how severely sick patients' mood got elevated when someone read aloud books to them. Study also revealed that epics, classics and poems are more effective. Interestingly, even the readers said they felt happy.

Pranic Healing & Reiki: I know quite a few who have undergone training in Pranic healing and they vouch for its effectiveness. Some of them shared that it is based on the principle of Karma and also on scientific principle of positive energy flow to unblock passages in the patient's body.

A friend shared that his father, 75 years, had relief through Pranic healing while undergoing Chemotherapy.

Acupressure/Acupuncture: *One of my family members got cured of frozen shoulder in 6 sittings whereas conventional medicines didn't offer lasting relief.*

Ayurvedic and Homeopathic treatments: While I know numerous cases of people getting treated and got pain relief, but there are also many who reported negligible or just temporary relief in spite of having spent large amount of money in high end detoxification resorts. It appears that it works wonders for some.

Hypnotism: I was amazed to watch Discovery Science, episode titled "Mind Control Freaks', when a hypnotist was able to create as well as mask pain in anyone at his will. Patients were able to undergo surgery without anaesthesia, under influence of Hypnotism.

Yoga: My yoga guru in Pune taught me that certain breathing techniques, like Anulom/Vilom, Kapabhati, and postures like Vajrasana could reduce pain.

Spiritual angle: A relative shared that she was able to reduce pain by disowning the body part that is in pain. For instance, when there was a pain in knee, she tells "that knee is in pain"- a modified version of what most people say "my knee is paining". This seems close to what Bhagwan Ramana Maharishi realised that 'he' is not his body.

———•●•———

Pain and Suffering are different – A valuable insight

"While Pain in body can be reduced only to some extent, there is no limit to reducing Suffering".

———•●•———

Pain and suffering are usually spoken together, often mistaken as inseparable. But it is not so. The difference and how to manage them are explained in ' Book of Joy' by Douglas Abrams, with co authors, Dalai Lama & Archbishop Desmond Tutu, as well as in ' The Art of Happiness' by Dalai Lama: The essence is given below:

Pain is a physiological process occurring at body level – when millions of sensory signals from the nerve endings travel to the base of brain. It is termed as a 'lower level process'. Pain can be reduced to varying levels, such as through medicines, therapies and surgeries. However all of these have limitations. Since any excessive, repetitive attempts to eliminate pain could be harmful, and that is more relevant to the aged due to possibility of serious side effects.

On the contrary, suffering is a psychological process occurring at the mental level, which is higher and more powerful than the body level. That is because, when pain signals reach the brain, at this juncture, the mind, based on its attitudes & emotions, developed over long time, assigns meaning and value.

Dr.Susan Babel, Psychologist, in "Emotions do Affect Chronic Pain", reveals that chronic pain can be caused by stress and emotional issues also.

In effect, the mind decides the quantum of suffering.

Control of suffering – Two Scenarios

Scenario 1: Mind Control 'Off'. Result – High suffering

Scenario 2: Mind Control 'On'. Result – Low suffering

The table below elaborates the distinction as well as the interconnectedness of pain and suffering, and possible solutions to alleviate them.

BODY PAIN	SUFFERING MIND	SOLUTION
Head	Stress	Relax. Meditate
Neck	Blame/ Grudge	Forgive. Love self & others
Shoulder	Unable to bear burden	Share burden with others.
Back	Unable to share; Yearn for appreciation	Share feelings. Take support.
Hands	Loneliness	Foster and nurture relationships
Hips	Fear of change. Indecisiveness	Plan and make small progress.
Knees/Calf	High expectations. Jealousy	Be realistic. Appreciate others.
Ankles / foot	Lethargy. Depression	Have purpose in life. Play with pet.

Additional tools and techniques to reduce suffering

The above findings and insights assure us that anyone can reduce/ eliminate suffering, and the way to do is further elaborates as under:

➢ *Spirituality*

- Being kind, supportive and compassionate.

- Trust in Guru/God/Higher Power.

- Belief in principle of Karma.

➢ *Mental Discipline*

- Shifting attention from self to others.

- Stopping worries by watching thoughts as a witness

- Overcoming Negativity; e.g. Fear, Guilt, Anger, Frustration, Stress, Also move away from people with negativity.

➢ *Attitude& Outlook*

- Grateful to available services & facilities.

- Optimism & Hope. Remind self with 'this too will pass'

- Developing an outlook that pain has value and useful.

➢ *Activities*

- Get out and volunteer to help others

- Involve in acts that bring peace and joy. E.g. Prayer; Meditation; Silence; Music; Reading; Writing etc.

➢ *Support:*

- Seek help from family and friends.

- Counselling from Professional.

—•—

True Stories of overcoming suffering

Faith in Karma/God: *During my childhood, on occasions of misfortunes, I used to hear the elders say "This suffering is due to my Karma". On some other instances, people would tell "God tests those who are close to him". Looking back, it seems they got solace due to such beliefs.*

A lady in mid 60's, diagnosed with a terminal illness shared "Great saints like Ramakrishna Paramahamsa and Ramana maharishi too had cancer. It means that all my remaining Karma is getting accelerated and getting extinguished in this birth itself. That means moksha is near". She appeared to be in peace.

Even Westerners, though not using the term Karma, seem to be aligned with its principles. For example, in "Man's Search for Meaning", Psychiatrist Dr. Viktor Frankl, while narrating tortuous experiences in Nazi camps, realised that *when a person derives a meaning from suffering, then he would be able to manage any level, never losing hope.*

Extra ordinary courage: I have come across many, while facing serious illness, have faced them with fortitude. When questioned from where and since when they became courageous, each one shared the same – they themselves were surprised about their resilience.

On introspection, I realise that just as investing small amount of money over a long period ends up in huge wealth, one's continual spiritual practice over many years, comes to rescue during times of personal crisis.

Being Grateful*: A woman, after diagnosed with cancer, and undergoing numerous tests, scans, chemotherapy and surgery, told me that her pain and suffering got drastically reduced after realising how fortunate she was to receive so much love and support from her husband, children, grand child, neighbours, siblings, as well as doctors, surgeons, the paramedical staff etc.*

On similar lines, during hospitalisation due to Covid 19, my friend's wife wrote a poem 'An ode to faceless beauties' as a token of gratitude to the doctors and staff.

Humour: *The woman with cancer (mentioned above) also shared that humour helped her in stressful situations. For example, just before mastectomy, the surgeon asked her "Are you confident madam?" to which she replied "I am. How about you?"*

Having a goal : *A woman, who suffered a stroke, shared: "The most important factor that helped me to recover was my goal - to see that my teenage son completes his university education, gets married and settles well in life".*

Value from misery: *My classmate, after diagnosed with Covid 19 and spending two weeks in hospital, on return to his home, told: "Earlier, I used to get hurt easily and quickly. Now I don't. Feelings of guilt are replaced by calmness. I suspect the two weeks that I spent with myself has brought about this change".*

Similarly, a neighbour shared that after a week of isolation in hospital, value of being with friends got reinforced.

Looking at the positive: A neighbour was *passionate about swimming and driving. But after suffering from epilepsy, he was advised by Neurologist to stop both. He was devastated, but quickly recovered, and said 'what if I had the epilepsy attack while swimming or driving? I could have died"*

Attitude matters: *When a relative was diagnosed with Parkinson's, he was asked by his son "Dad, I know you have been religious and honest throughout your life. Didn't you ask God, 'Why me?' when you were told about this incurable disease. The father replied "Throughout my life, I have always been blessed with the best. I never asked God 'why me, then. How can I, now?"*

Modified mindset*: My wife and I visited a friend who had undergone a major surgery. She said "I am praying to God to give me strength to overcome this suffering". After a pause, my wife remarked "If you ask for strength, it means you don't have it now. Instead, you thank God for having given you the strength already". The friend realised the value and agreed to change her mind set.*

Prayer*: Terry Anderson, American journalist, was kidnapped in Beirut in 1985, imprisoned and tortured till 1991. After release, when asked how did he manage, and from where did he get the strength to survive, he replied "my regular prayers".*

Dr. Larry Dossy in 'Healing Words' says prayer is one of the best kept secrets in medical science.

Meditation: An Doo, from Taiwan, in 'Meditation and Health', shared " When other forms of medications failed, I began practicing Bodhi Meditation, which gave immense relief from chronic back ache, pain in eyes and weight reduction; even my family life and relationships improved".

Support & Sharing*: An incident narrated by a CEO in 'The art of happiness': "I went into depression after failure in my new venture. Drugs offered only short time relief. Then, for the first time, I shared my problems with my wife. She listened and offered me emotional support. I overcame depression without medications".*

———◆———

Illness

"Firstly have a strong will and mind not to fall ill. Secondly push peace into every cell of your body, enjoining them not to be afraid. Then think & do something else"

- The Mother, Sri Aurobindo ashram in 'The Sunlit Path'.

———•———

Planning a visit to a Doctor/Hospital

(Source: Reader's Digest, December 2016):

Being organised, making adequate preparations before meeting a doctor/getting admitted to hospital can help in getting prompt and improved medical attention as explained below:

- Ensure adequate medical Insurance coverage, including towards serious ailments, surgeries and prolonged hospitalisation.

- Get a prior appointment with the Doctor/Hospital to reduce waiting time.

- Plan your trip to reach in time.

- Take all necessary documents including prescriptions, test reports, files etc

- Doctors are busy. Go with a written down list of all doubts, fears.

- Raise the doubts that were noted. Write down the answers if needed.

- When Doctor's prescriptions are not legible, write them in capital letters on back side

- Since elders are more vulnerable to side effects, if any new medicine is prescribed, ask if there could be any side effects. Also inform the medicines you already take; and tell him if you are aware of any allergies.

- If Doctor advises surgery, inform him if you plant to get a second opinion.

- Get Doctor's or the hospital's emergency numbers to contact when needed.

- Both the patient and the doctor have certain rights and responsibilities, including: right to information, courtesy, privacy, confidentiality, safety, and grievance resolution. Be aware of them and adhere to them.

Importance of a family physician

- There used to be a tradition of having a family physician, who would be aware of physical and emotional aspects of all members of a family. He also would be a trusted family member and a counsellor, available on 24 x 7. Unfortunately, this tradition has eroded.

- As a consequence, many, including elders directly approach several specialists, who work in 'water tight compartments', get treated in piece-meal basis, thereby missing a holistic, integrated treatment. Worse, the mutual trust is also declining.

- In major illnesses, the second opinion from a specialist could contradict the one by the first, and on some occasions, the patient is asked to make the decision as if he is the specialist.

- Therefore, the absence of a trusted, competent family physician poses many risks, including conflicting medications that could create serious side effects, unwarranted, repeated tests & procedures, wasteful expenditures; higher physical and mental stress etc.

Those who don't have a family physician, it is still possible to utilise one's contacts, assess, and finalise one. I have done that in spite of several relocations.

Role of Geriatrician

(Source: "Elders Well Being" in 'National Alliance of Seniors Association', Chennai):

Various health risks which were detailed earlier could be effectively managed by understanding the role of a Geriatrician – one who specialises in treatment of elders with comprehensive & holistic care in physical, psychological, cognitive and social functions. His focus is to improve or sustain or prevent further deterioration in quality of life of a senior as far as possible. Unlike a General Physician, he also gives attention to the care givers.

When should an elder consult a Geriatrician? When experiencing any of the following symptoms:

- Sudden difficulty or inability to perform daily routine functions.

- Abrupt drop in walking speed

- Memory loss

- Any suspicion of dementia, depression etc.

Risks in medications for elders

"For elders, when a drug is prescribed and taken, it works as a medicine. On the contrary, when any drug is consumed without prescription, then it can even become a poison". – Dr.V.S.Natarajan, Geriatrician, Chennai

Polypharmacy risk: Many elders could have several ailments and so they take multiple medicines – this risk is known as 'Polypharmacy', says Dr. Naresh Bhatt, CMI, Bangalore, because one drug might adversely affect functioning of another. Importantly, the risk of Polypharmacy increases with the number of drugs being taken. The risk can be reduced by sharing the details of all the medicines being taken while consulting any Physician, as mentioned earlier.

Misleading symptoms and self medication risks

(Source: Dr V S Natarajan, Geriatrician, in 'Elders … Well being')

- Compared to youngsters, elders show vast differences in their responses to even common medicines.

- Hence, they should strictly avoid self medication, including taking pain killers* for long duration due to several risks including kidney failure.

- Symptoms of the aged people are more difficult to diagnose; e.g. one may suffer heart attack but pain could appear in abdomen and not in chest.

- Dosage should not be altered without consulting a doctor.

- Medicines prescribed for one should not be taken by anyone else.

- Medicines should not be stopped without consultation.

*On pain killers, following question and answer appeared in a magazine:

Question by a 75+: For my knee pain, I took a pain killer. Immediately I developed stomach pain, then vomited blood and got hospitalized. Why so?

Answer by Geriatrician: This self medication could have even killed you. Vomiting blood is due to pain killer causing ulcers in stomach, about which you were unaware of. For the aged, many diseases don't give any symptoms at all, and so even if you take Over The Counter (OTC) medicines that does not need any prescription, that too could be dangerous, due to your age factor.

Medicine Safety- Recommended Practices

- For each person, keep medicines at different places to prevent mix up.

- Different medicines may be kept in different coloured boxes, for each.

- Alarms can be set on mobile to remind medicine intake.

- While purchasing medicines, check they are as per prescription and expiry date is ok.

- Destroy out dated medicines.

- For regular medicines, keep stock for 2 to 3 weeks.

Hospitalisation – Recommendations, Challenges and True Stories

Hospital Atmosphere: In a TED talk, "Death and Architecture", Alison King observes: "Stays in hospitals are getting longer due to increased availability of health care benefits and longevity. So, the hospital atmosphere for the sick should get better with an ambience that is pleasant, cheerful, sunny, airy, lively and ergonomically designed.

I was pleasantly surprised to notice an atrium with lots of greenery in the centre of a hospital in Coimbatore and I felt a sudden rise in my mood as I stepped in.

Networking: Personally knowing a doctor (either directly or through contacts) in a hospital is of immense help for quick admission, better personal attention, getting a second opinion and even discounts on billing. Obviously, such networking need to be made before the necessity arises.

Other day, an elder had a fall, and his wife rushed him to a multi speciality hospital. Their daughter, living in another city ensured her father got immediate consultation, tests, found no serious injury, was discharged within half a day. I believe that for anyone else without such contacts, this process could have been longer.

Fear and overcoming it: Everyone, not just elders is afraid of hospitalisation. Key reasons are: stress, pain, threat of immobility, expenditures, even fear of death.

Even getting into an ambulance is scary for some. One elder refused to get into it, and insisted that she should be taken to the hospital in a normal vehicle. Later, she clarified "a ride in an ambulance appeared as my last journey".

But there are exceptions.

A woman (90), agreed for surgery, even after being told by the surgeon that the success rate is only 60%. She told him "I would rather die once rather than undergo pain and death every moment". Her eventual recovery was 90%, the reason being her courage according to the surgeon.

Another friend (male, 69), and a relative (female, 66), were diagnosed with cancer. Both shared that they were surprised by the courage they had shown throughout the long period that involved numerous consultations, tests, multiple surgeries followed by therapies. Now, both are leading normal lives. Interestingly, all the three referred above became role models and counsellors to other patients.

Involving patients: Often, the elderly patients are not kept fully informed about the details of illness. Though this is done with the good intention so as to not create stress, ironically, in some cases, it could act otherwise. It seems some level of discretion is needed.

A neighbour, who suffered a stroke and hospitalised, noticed her husband used to have long discussions with doctors, but she was not kept informed. She summed up "I felt it was like a stab on my individuality".

Behavioural Changes: As mentioned earlier, some demonstrate altered (deteriorated) behaviour, during hospitalisation. These include: becoming abusive, being adamant, increased irritableness, non-cooperation etc.

Such behavioural changes are attributed to:

- Frustration arising out of difficulties in carrying out day to day tasks, leading to dependence on others.

- Disappointments if expected support didn't come from Children/ Relatives/Friends.

A woman (80+) after a fall and head injury was advised by Neurologist not to spend too much time on small screens-mobile &TV. But she disobeyed, creating much stress to her Children.

A man (85+), who was known to be calm and composed, began to abuse his wife, his sole care giver after admission to an ICU. His behaviour returned to normalcy after improvement in his health. Interestingly, he could not believe when told about his bad conduct during his illness.

Such behavioural changes are mostly unintentional and temporary, and once the elder recovers, he returns to former/normal behaviour. This knowledge is useful for caregivers so that they could consciously practice patience and tolerance.

Recovery after Hospitalisation: Norman Cousins, editor of 'Saturday Review', fell critically ill in 1964, and doctors told him that there is no chance of full recovery. Norman, however recovered fully, and attributed following reasons for it:

- A strong purpose to live to serve humanity.

- Courage and perseverance to fight the disease.

- Owning up responsibility for cure & recovery.

- Changed attitude to pain by realising its value.

- Trust in the body & mind in their healing & regenerative powers.

- Relationship with the Physician based on trust, care & openness

- Becoming knowledgeable about the illness, treatment; asking questions to get clarifications on any doubts.

- Hygienic hospital; balanced & nutritious diet; caring & competent staff; peaceful & conducive environment

- Consciously developing positive emotions, including cheerfulness, humour, optimism and gratefulness.

Counselling - A missing link

The practice of counselling a patient is widely practiced in western countries. More than 20 years ago, when I was living in Netherlands, I learnt that they counsel even those who happen to witness a serious accident. Regrettably this process is still missing in India as per my discussion with a Physician who has large number of seniors among his patients. He observed "There is no change in attitude of even highly educated, who tend to believe that only people who are 'mad' should visit a counsellor. It's still a social stigma. While everyone rushes to a doctor on the silliest problem with body, but, when it comes to even serious illness of mind, no one opts for counselling. Yes, even Physicians do not recommend though they should encourage it".

I also witnessed that even reputed hospitals assign counsellors work other than counselling, so patients and care givers manage on their own.

Caregivers – The ignored lot:

"During my hospitalisation, I realised that it was not just me, but all my family members too were sufferers"

– A woman who underwent prolonged hospitalisation.

Awareness that those who take care of the sick also undergo stress, mental as well as physical, is low. I too became conscious about it only recently after watching and discussing with several people. In cases where the care giver is also a senior, which is on the rise in recent years, then, that person's stress could become even higher than the patient.

A man (75+) told "I felt I grew older by ten years in a single year, when I, all alone had to take care of my sick wife".

In another instance, a woman (70+) shared "I have been taking care of my father, who is 93 now, for the last twenty years. But, over the last four years, he has become increasingly abusive; he repeatedly shouts at me for no obvious reasons. As I am also getting old, I am unable to bear this stress".

Perhaps an extreme case of stress in a care giver, a woman (70+) said about her sick mother (90) "Taking her to hospital has become too frequent and I am no longer able to bear that strain. I feel ashamed to say this but a thought came to me last time that hopefully this time she will not return home..."

Visitors to Hospital: They have responsibility to ensure that what they say, how they behave leave a positive impact on the patient. Unsolicited advice, spreading mis information should be avoided. Besides, a patient's privacy should be understood and respected.

-----•-----

Managing Terminal Stage & Letting Go

Status of a patient: How sick is a patient? How close is he to death? These are questions that arise in the minds of a patient (if he is mentally alert) and his family members. The chart below, known as Karnofsky score, though meant for doctors to identify the type and level of therapies needed, offers clues.

Score	Interpretation
100	Normal. No evidence of disease
90	Able to do normal activity. Minor symptoms of disease
80	Normal activity, but with effort. Some symptoms of disease
70	Difficulty to do normal activity.
60	Requires occasional assistance
50	Requires considerable assistance & frequent medical care
40	Disabled. Requires special care.
30	Severely disabled.
20	Hospitalisation. Active supportive treatment.
10	Moribund. Death imminent
0	Death

***

Prolonged hospitalisation: With increasing longevity, improving medical science, growing affordability, more people spend longer durations in hospitals. While some hospitals seem to be quite pleased to keep them, others are honest enough to inform the family that there is no hope of survival of the patient.

***

Letting Go

The Mother of Sri Aurobindo ashram Pondicherry in 'The sunlit path' observes " During the last moments of life on earth, when the vital Being and body is still united, the dying person's last hopes, aspirations, desires, attachments have immense importance for the Being. Following are the two important dimensions:

First: If the dying person could get rid of attachments (to people and material), then his Being would find it easy to free from body. If not, he undergoes a terrible battle within.

Second: There is a great responsibility on the family too. They should not cling (to the patient) for selfish reasons or due to their own attachments. These two approaches can help the 'Being' to leave the body, and enter into higher consciousness easily.

Corroborating the above by the Mother was a narration by a woman (70+): "My husband was in last phase of his life. But, I realised that he was deeply worried about something that prevented his soul leaving the body. Then I recollected what he shared a few years ago after he suffered heart attack – his concern was how I would manage finances, and whether I could get along well with my two daughters in law. After that insight, I got my two sons and their spouses, who were living abroad, to visit and reassure my husband with sign & body languages (as he lost hearing by then) that they would take care of me and the money matters, that he need not have any concerns. He seemed to understand, which was evident from his facial expression. Subsequently, I made it a practice to regularly hold his hands and whisper in his ears that I love him, will always do so, and that's why I don't want him to suffer any longer. I also assured him that I am in safe hands of our loving Children. Over a period of about fortnight, I noticed that his frown was slowly vanishing; his face gradually became serene; he passed away peacefully in sleep".

I have heard several similar stories about terminally ill patients, who had deep attachments or worries find difficulty in leaving this world. In such cases, if the spouse or children or someone else identified those issues and offer assurance, take corrective actions, then the misery is not prolonged and peaceful end comes.

Palliative Care: This is an interdisciplinary medical care and the treatment plan is from the time of diagnosis of a serious advanced illness through end of life. Focus is at reducing pain, mitigating suffering, and improving quality of life. Permanent cure is usually not expected but believe that pain need not always be part of dying.

Hospice Care: For terminally ill patients, Hospice care focuses to reduce pain and suffering, looking into emotional and spiritual needs at the end of life.

A friend (73) shared her experience: "My husband, who had history of heart ailments, suddenly fell very sick, and spent seven weeks in a hospital. Then the doctors told me that he has no chance of recovery, and I should either take him home or to a hospice care. This means I am letting my husband of 45 years to die. I was horrified. Though I have been watching him undergoing endless pain and suffering, I could not accept his end. When I consulted my relative who is a doctor, she agreed with the recommendation of the hospital. Slowly I reconciled to my husband's death as I didn't want him to suffer more pain. I moved him to a hospice where his end came peacefully after three weeks".

When Death is quickened

Factors that quicken one's end are:

Loss: Most would have come across instances when a partner dies, the other too follows soon. Scientific studies across the world too have proven that loss of a life partner quickens the death of spouse

Separation: Refers to separation from a person that a patient is strongly attached to.

A friend shared that her 90 year old mother's health deteriorated radically and died soon after her grandson left abroad for higher studies.

Relocation: Moving out of home in which one has been living for long (often for many decades) can be devastating.

A neighbour told that her father's health suddenly deteriorated when he was forced to relocate from his home of 34 years.

Loss of Will to Live: Some reach this phase, after which any medical treatment seem to be of no use.

An acquaintance shared that his father (91) didn't have any major health issues. Their family physician too told that all his vital organs are in good condition. But he told family members that there is no will to live. Thereafter, he began to vomit any type of food. Within about six months, he passed away.

Unbearable Pain: When there seems to be no cure for pain, some elders wish for death. A few get into depression and even commit suicide.

Do-Not-Resuscitate (DNR): This is a legal practice signed by a person, on his own accord, while in good mental health, declaring that he does not wish to receive 'Cardio Pulmonary Resuscitation (CPR); he may also specify denial of other medical interventions. The legal document needs to be countersigned by a Physician, based on medical judgement, the person's wishes and values. DNR is prevalent in some Western countries, while in India it has just begun to get noticed and practiced.

A friend (69) told that her father had signed DNR, when he was 90 years and reasonably healthy. When he turned 94 and fell seriously ill, lost interest to live, he refused hospitalisation or any artificial life saving devices, and passed away at home.

Advance Medical Directive (AMD): Also referred to as 'A living will', AMD is similar to DNR – a legal document, prepared and signed in advance, when an elder is in good mental health. It specifies a person's wishes regarding medical treatment, specifically one that aims to prolong life, through various devices. To prevent its misuse, the Supreme Court has laid down guidelines for its execution.

Essentially, both DNR and AMD aim to serve the following:

- Upholding the right to die with dignity, while reducing pain and suffering.

- Helps medical professionals to take tough decisions during terminal stages

- Frees the patient's family/care giver from guilt and litigations.

Organ Donation*: A noble act that is recommended. Besides* donating eyes (corneas), in case of 'brain dead', one can donate most other organs as well. Many hospitals accept advance registration. After doing so, the Children/care giver/family physician should be kept informed.

My wife and I have registered for donation of all our organs.

———•••———

Summary: Pain, Illness, hospitalisation & last phase:

> *Pain has huge value and is different from suffering.*

> *Pain emanating from body can be reduced only to a certain extent, but suffering arising at mind has no limit for alleviation.*

> *Self medication is risky for anyone, but seniors are at very high risk. Hence, they should take any medicine only with prescription.*

> *Trust both: Natural healing powers of the body & the doctor.*

> *There are many ways to be at peace during the last stage of life*

MANAGING LOSS, BEREAVEMENT & GRIEF

. . . .

"While I was in Nazi's prison, I realised that true love goes beyond the physical presence of the loved one. That is true even if that person is not alive"

– Viktor Frankl in 'Man's Search for Meaning'

MANAGING LOSS OF A LOVED ONE

The biggest fear for anyone is loss - of spouse, children, grand child, sibling, a close relative or a friend.

This fear reached a new high during the Covid 19 pandemic for elderly parents living away from Children. Unfortunately many don't possess the necessary skills to manage loss. This chapter attempts to offer clues to manage it.

The five stages: Most would know the theory of the five stages of grief identified by Elisabeth Kübler-Ross (1926 – 2004), a Swiss-American psychiatrist. Though it was originally intended for the terminally ill, later it was adopted to those who have lost their loved ones too. Understanding these five steps given below could help in handling the loss better:

Stage	Feeling	Behaviour
1	Denial	Tries to deny what happened
2	Anger	Asks repeatedly "Why Me?"
3	Bargain	Pleads, prays to God to reverse the event.
4	Depression	Tendency towards depression
5	Acceptance	With time, bereaved accepts the reality / loss

How Indians manage loss: (*Source: Report by Tata Institute of Social Science (TISS), Mumbai).*

- Most Indians don't know how to cope with grief including loss.

- Death of spouse, child or grandchild is most traumatic.

- Grieving behaviour of women and men are usually different.

  ○ Women are more intuitive, experience more feelings of sorrow, guilt, and depression. So they are more vulnerable.

  ○ Men usually do not know how to handle grief. Many just get into action mode, diverting their mind to doing various tasks.

- Teaching how to manage money is the vital support needed for a woman who lost her husband.

Crying helps: Dr. Stephen Sideroff, a clinical psychologist at UCLA, USA, reports: "Crying activates the body in a healthy way. It is a very positive, healthy thing to do. While stress tightens muscles and heightens tension, but when one cries, some of that tension gets released".

A related insight is that emotional tears contain higher levels of stress hormones, and more of mood regulating mineral manganese, compared to tears that are meant for lubricating or reflex.

On using crying to de-stress, the Japanese have even formed crying clubs called 'rui-katsu' (means "tear-seeking"). To help develop tears they screen sad, tear jerking movies!

So, when sad or bereaved, one should not hesitate to cry. That applies to men too, who feel embarrassed to shed tears due to the wrong notion that 'men should not cry'.

This also means that while trying to console a bereaved one, no need to advice 'don't cry' or 'stop crying'.

'Emotional Debt': A term coined by David Viscott, Psychiatrist, who found connection between faster ageing and stored- up sorrow. This reinforces the need to grieve and not suppress emotion of loss.

I cried on death of my mother after 35 years! True to the finding of TISS, Mumbai (mentioned earlier), when my ailing mother breathed last, my mind was so preoccupied with the hundreds of tasks that I needed to manage that I didn't mourn much, instead got into action mode. Long after that, as I was writing an article about her simple and yet unfulfilled desires, I broke down inconsolably in the presence of my wife and son. I finally grieved the loss of my mother after three and half decades.

Suggestions from Dalai Lama: In 'Art of Happiness', he offers several useful tips to overcome grief as follows:

- Belief in rebirth gives consolation

- When a bereaved becomes more compassionate, particularly to those who had undergone similar losses, it brings solace.

— •●•—

Advice from Counsellors: During the Pandemic, I participated in many Webinars on the topic of "How to manage loss", which was conducted by reputed hospitals in collaboration with Counsellors. The essence of them is given below.

Legend: Problem posed by a participant is denoted as **(P)** followed by age and gender. Advice by Counsellor is denoted as **(A):**

P by 70+ male: I feel guilty for death of my wife since I was the one who passed on the corona virus to her.

A: It was the virus that killed your wife and not you. Also you would never know for sure who passed on the virus. So there is no need for you to feel guilty.

P by 40+ male: I lost my father, and I don't know how to console my aged mother.

A: Make a habit of spending some time with her every day. Just your presence with her will console. It is not always necessary that you should say something. In fact, it's better *not* to philosophise.

P by 75+ male: I suspect I am under depression after death of my wife.

A: Are you able to do your day to day/routine functions, after two/three weeks of death of your wife? If not, it's better to seek professional help.

P by 80+ female: I still feel sad and cannot forget my husband even after a year of his death.

A: Sadness will be there. There is no need to forget him to overcome sadness. You can pursue your interests, do community work that your husband was passionate about. That could help reducing your grief.

P by 70+ male: My nephew, 53 year old, died of Covid. It is two months now and I am yet to overcome this loss. I have stopped interacting with people and going out.

A: Do not withdraw yourself. Return to normal routine at the earliest. If you are unable to do so, seek counselling.

—•—•—

Interdependence aggravates: Another factor that increases grief was identified by Harvard psychologist David McClelland, which is 'when love and relationships are based on interdependence – which is also a kind of selfishness – then the bereaved undergoes higher suffering'.

Loser to Winner: Swami Dayananda Saraswati counsels that loss has value, and it is crucial that the bereaved does not lose it. By finding a value, a 'loser' becomes a 'winner' in the most profound sense.

Two decades ago, when I was in Pune, a Swamiji met me and asked "Can you recognise me?" I couldn't. He continued "I am Rahul, Civil engineering consultant. I worked in your project three years ago". I then recognised the face behind the beard, and asked "Why have you become a sanyasi?" He narrated his story "Two years ago, I lost my only son in a road accident. He was just 29 years. My wife and I were devastated. How can God punish me – an honest, sincere, religious man? I decided to find the reason. So I travelled across India, stayed in ashrams, met many Gurus, but didn't get a convincing answer. Finally, the breakthrough came when I met a Guru, here, in Pune itself. He, over several sessions, explained and made me understand the Law of Karma. I contemplated, realised its value, overcame my grief, and got peace of mind. Now I am helping others under similar situations".

'Wabi-sabi': This is a Japanese term, which means appreciating imperfections and understanding that nothing is permanent in day to day life. For example, not getting too much upset when one's precious crockery is broken. If this principle gets gradually ingrained, then even a loss of a dear one could be borne with less grief and more equanimity.

'Antifragile': This is a term describing a quality of being resilient while facing any crisis including loss, and importantly, becoming stronger than ever before.

I have come across many, including a few in my family, who have been able to accomplish this.

Second-Innings: As mentioned in the earlier chapter on Companionship, there is increasing acceptance from Children and the society, towards marriage between elders who are single, also termed ' Second Innings'. This is an option to overcome loneliness following loss of spouse.

— • —

True stories on facing loss

"My wife is always with me": A friend's sharing *"My wife died inside the aircraft during our flight to USA. I didn't know how to handle* *this emergency. But unexpected support came from strangers - the flight crew, ground staff, Indian consulate and the Indian community at the next scheduled stop over– such acts of kindness softened my shock. It took me two years to overcome the grief, thanks to support from my daughter, son in law, friends and neighbours. Later, my behaviour also changed for better - from self pity and frequent bursts of crying to being patient and compassionate. Reading Bhagwad Gita, chanting Gayatri mantra offered solace. While eating, if there is any dish which is my wife's favourite, I would keep that aside for her, because I feel she is always with me.*

"My mother never left me": *Narration by an acquaintance: "You may not believe but whenever I open my mother's cupboard filled with her sarees and personal effects, I sense her body aroma, which makes me feel her presence. It seems my mother never left me".*

"Her Presence in All": *My friend's son wrote the following piece on passing away of his grandmother. Its extract: "'My Nani (grandma) moved out of our home with a smiling, serene countenance. Shocked, insecure and sad, I looked up at the sky for solace. I sensed her presence in the sunrays, clouds, breeze….everywhere. I regained my security and joy. After a while, a doubt arose – is my feeling a mere imagination? Frankly I don't know. But, what I do know is - I am filled with love and peace for my Nani. Nothing else matters".*

"I will reunite": *Another friend's story: "When my wife died, the immediate support from my brother in law helped me to a large extent to bear the initial shock. Then, I diverted my attention to serving the poor - I took care of the watchman and his family who resided in our housing complex. Besides, I have developed a new habit". He showed photo of his wife and continued. "When I get up in the morning, I say 'Good Morning', followed by 'I love you' to my wife. Whenever I step out of my house, I inform her where I am going and when I will return". Then he led me to the* *puja room, pointed to a brass urn covered with orange cloth and continued "That contains ashes of my wife. I have written in my Will that after my death, my ashes should be mixed with hers and immersed in the Ganges, so I will re-unite with her, forever".*

"She is always with me"

"He is happy with Him": *Another person said "I know for sure that my husband is now with the God, enjoying His Love. Why should I feel sad?"*

"Found a new purpose": *This man lost his wife and daughter within a span of two years. He explained how he coped "I was devastated. After death of my spouse, my daughter and I used to make weekly visits to a day care centre for those suffering from Alzheimer's. Then after demise of my daughter, I began to visit the centre more frequently as a loving tribute to my daughter. When those inmates remember and praise my daughter's kindness, I get peace. I have found a new purpose in life".*

"Changed perspective": *In a reunion, I was consoling my friend, who lost his son. When I asked him how he coped, he responded "Yes, I was distressed. Then I changed my outlook. I told myself that I was fortunate to have a wonderful son for 35 years. That perspective transformed grief to gratitude".*

"Awaiting her call": *I met a neighbour (80+) at his home. On knowing the purpose of my visit, he looked up at his wife's picture hung on the wall and narrated "She was a house wife for a while, but later, she studied, became a school teacher, and rose to become the Head mistress. She was kind, supported the poor students. In spite of all these, God took her away, due to my Karma. Just before her death, she promised me that she would call me. I am waiting……".*

"Loss brought me relief": *When I called my friend (70) to condole after demise of his mother (91), he said "I am relieved, since if she had survived me, there is no one to look after her"*

———•◆•———

Summary: Managing Loss and Bereavement

- ✓ ***Strengthening spirituality helps in managing loss.***

- ✓ ***"Love for any person is within oneself. So, physical presence (of that person) is not necessary - From Hindu scriptures***

- ✓ ***There are many ways to manage loss.***

- ✓ ***If one is unable to manage a loss even after about three months, then, the bereaved is recommended to seek professional help.***

DEATH - A PROMISING NEW BEGINNING

Both in Life and Death, God is equally present.

Be aware and see Him

– Swami Vivekananda

It is said that a river trembles with fear before entering a sea. As the sea is new and vast, the river is afraid of losing its identity. It feels comfortable while looking at the familiar path it travelled. But going back is against nature. The only way for it to overcome its fear is to enter the sea. Soon, realisation comes that by merging, the river has become an ocean – a promising new beginning.

– Adapted from 'Fear' by Khalil Gibran

FEAR OF DEATH

Most people, irrespective of their age, are 'mortally' scared of death. Though that is well known, yet, I would like to narrate a few incidents.

While researching for this book, I used to discuss the various topics with some of my friends. Whenever I mentioned that one of the chapters is 'Death', most recoiled, many were visibly disturbed, and a few suggested that I should drop that subject, justifying with "How death can be a chapter in a book about happiness?"

I got to know that the fear of death is high even among elders, when I picked a CD about Death in a library located in a Seniors Community Living, and noticed that its original wrapper was intact!

On similar lines, I read the following incident narrated by a woman in an English magazine: "My father always used to visit the temple in our locality on his birthday every year. But when he turned 93, he refused to do so for the first time. After prolonged probing, he sheepishly confessed 'I am afraid that when I visit the temple, God will notice and call me up'

A woman (90+), after becoming terminally ill, used to insist that her husband, three sons, daughters in law and grand children to be near her always, that all the lights should be 'on', as she believed these would drive away Yama, the Lord of Death.

I have had discussions with many whose parents passed away at 90 years and above, including one at 101. I asked each one of them "Did your parent manage to overcome the fear of death? " Everyone said "No".

And then the Covid 19 Pandemic gave ample opportunities to observe people's behaviour and fears about death. It confirmed my doubt and I came to a conclusion that 'fear of death increases with age'.

That insight also re-enforced my view that I should write about death, and suggest ways to reduce the fear associated with it.

Overcoming the fear of death

"Everybody likes to go to heaven. But nobody wants to die"

– Steve Jobs (1955/2011) Co-founder of Apple Inc

Following are some suggestions drawn from various sources that could help to overcome, or at least reduce the fear of death.

Belief in Karma and Reincarnation to overcome fear of death

Studying, contemplating and trusting on Karma & Reincarnation helps in reducing the fear of death. Given below is the essence extracted from several books on the Hindu scriptures, combined with my reasoning:

- For a Soul (Atman) to fulfil its desires, it needs a body with sense organs. But the body has limited life and dies, and then the Soul acquires a new body (birth) to enjoy the unfulfilled pleasures/ attain remaining aspirations.

- But there is a time gap (different scale than on earth) between a Soul's cycle of leaving a body and then re-entering another. During this time gap, the Soul, based on its accumulated Karma, enters astral plane (Lok) where it can upgrade its talent and achieve a creative leap. After completion of its term in the 'Lok', soul returns to earth, carrying not only the accumulated talent of all the previous births, but also upgraded talent which was acquired in the astral plane after it left the last body. The soul then seeks the most favourable circumstances that would facilitate it to further upgrade its talent and enters a body. This principle is logical and aligned with science and evolution; it also explains the phenomenon of child prodigies.

- This cycle continues till a Soul's Karma account becomes nil, (i.e. all desires, aspirations are extinguished, so there is no more any need for a body). The Soul is now said to be liberated.

- The liberated Soul, its inherent nature being pure bliss, timeless and indestructible, unites with the God/'Super Consciousness'/'Paramatma'/attain 'moksha' or whatever name one may give.

On reincarnation, there have been several studies including by the Westerners. For example, Prof. Ian Stevenson, University of Virginia has identified, verified, and documented hundreds of cases of reincarnation across the world.

The Mother (Aurobindo Ashram, Pondicherry) also narrates an incident:"Whenever we assembled for meditation, a cat named Kiki would come promptly, on each and every occasion, sit always on an arm chair, and go into a trance (not sleeping). It seemed to me that Kiki had aspirations to become a human in its next life".

Similar to above was an incident reported in an English national daily - a stray dog joined a man who was part of a group of pilgrims who were walking from Bangalore to Sabarimala. When that man died on the way and the group abandoned their trip, this dog then joined another group and never left them till it reached near the temple when it was not allowed to go any further - a distance of about 400 Kms, which lasted about eight days. Highly inspired, one pilgrim adopted the dog and took it to his home in Bangalore.

My wife and I too experienced an incident similar to the above. During our morning walks on public roads, she used to listen to Vishnu Sahasranamam played from her mobile. One day, as the chanting began, a stray dog, which was sleeping on the road side, got up and began to follow her. It left her immediately when the recital ended. This incident repeated for about a month. In between, we conducted a few experiments - halted mid way and changed the directions, but the dog never left her till the closure of the chanting. Our above experience cum experiment had to be abandoned due to outbreak of Corona when we stopped going out. Like the Kiki the cat which never failed to attend meditation, the stray dog that walked 400 Kms to reach a holy shrine, we also believe that the street dog had aspirations to be born a human- sometime in the future.

Learning from sages & true events to conquer fear of death

Thiruvalluvar (31 BCE, Tamil Poet and Sage), in Kural 339 says: "Death and birth are like going to sleep and waking up"

Two decades ago, my yoga guru in Pune, taught 'Yoga Nidhra' and Meditation, and said "You can experience death even while being alive by observing the moment when you are about to fall asleep. Also practice meditation. In both these cases, you come close to experiencing death, because the mind and body seem separated for a while, and so you can overcome the fear of death". I am practicing these, and hope to succeed before it's too late.

More clarity emerges from the experience shared by Bhagwan Ramana Maharishi (1879/1950, Tiruvannamalai, Tamil Nadu). Its essence: "I was about 16 years then, and though I had no health issues, a sudden fear of death overtook me. I felt I am going to die and enquired 'What is dying? What happens after this body is cremated? Am I the body?' I realised that 'I' am not my body because I was able to feel the force and voice of 'I' within me –a Spirit which is deathless. Then the fear of death vanished, once for all. Sleep is like death but temporary, while death is just longer sleep. Meditation and silence will drive away the fear of death'

One can also get inspired by many sages who have voluntarily opted for death, specifying the date and time, even while their bodies are in good health, which is known as 'Jeeva Samadhi', in which case the Praan (life force) leaves a healthy body voluntarily (note: this is *not* suicide). On the contrary, for the rest of us, the Praan is forced to leave a sick body after all its vital organs fail.

On similar lines, some Tibetan monks follow 'Bardo Thodal' (means the art of dying) in which the dying person is helped to relax by making him chant or make him listen to chanting by other monks. The dying monk becomes a witness to his death. When done in that manner, dying and death become a beautiful experience. The Jain Munis call similar practice as 'Sallekhana'. Prasannamati Mataji, a Jain nun said "Death is full of excitement and novel possibilities – like visiting a new, beautiful place. Hence you can embrace death not out of disappointment with existing life, but to gain something new and more meaningful experience"

More on above is the story shared by my friend: "When my father turned 70, though he was healthy, he handed over family responsibilities to my eldest brother. He then began to spend time in service at a nearby temple. When he turned 74, he called all of us, and told that his responsibilities in this birth are over, and so, has decided to leave his body. He stopped eating, and later drinking water too. He remained calm and composed and passed away peacefully in about a week".

Power of Oneness: Realising that one is not an isolated individual but intricately connected with every living being – feeling of interconnectedness and Oneness can help. Albert Einstein said "I feel so much a part of all forms of life that I am not concerned with beginning and end of me or any particular person".

Dying and Death can be peaceful: Palliative care specialist Seamus Coyle, in the BBC's Future series in 'Death - Can our final moments be euphoric?' cited a few examples where, persons in final moments seem to be in peace and harmony. This is also supported by a post from a Swedish (in the same series) "Just after death, most look as if they are sleeping. In fact, a relative of mine, who had intense pain before death, had a radiant expression after his death"

I still vividly recall death of my mother though it happened forty four years ago. During her last moments, her head was on my lap; I watched her eyes slowly going up; breathing slowed down and then stopped. I witnessed death so closely. And even after so many years, I remember her serene face after death.

Power of visualisation: A woman (65+) shared that she has been visualising her death in which her Guru, Shirdi Sai Baba is with her during her last moments, and after her death, he escorts her Spirit to be with him forever. She felt that her fear of death has considerably reduced after such repeated visualisations.

Visualising a peaceful death with Guru/favourite God can reduce the fear

---

'Out of Body Experience' OBE/'Near Death Experience' NDE: These have been studied and documented on numerous occasions, across several countries, over many decades and they give hope that death need not be a painful experience. Following are the most common elements: A person is in a critical health condition; he is near death or even declared dead. His Spirit leaves the body, but it is able to see its body like a third person, and can notice people around. The spirit then watches its life's events as a quick flashback. During that time, its favourite God or Guru or a dead close family member is nearby. While watching it, spirit also experiences the associated emotions, but mostly in a non-traumatic way. It then travels through a tunnel, at the end of which, sees a powerful but soothing, loving light. At this juncture, it gets 'communicated' that its time on earth has not ended, and so, should return. The spirit then re-enters the body, and comes back to life. Most reported that OBE has been peaceful.

New Experiences: Since death is never experienced while alive, by undergoing new experiences, one may be able to reduce the fear about it.

These can be even in day to day activities like - taking different routes and directions in daily walks; travelling to un known destinations; talking to strangers etc.

Being Prepared: As mentioned earlier, death can be faced with ease when the causes of unwillingness of 'Praan' to live a body can be identified and resolved. This can be done when worries and anxieties of the dying person are identified and resolved. For example, in many senior couples, the wife is ignorant on money matters, while the husband knows little about domestic affairs. So, being prepared for all such eventualities would facilitate Spirit leaving a terminally sick body with ease.

Since retirement, I have identified such areas of concern, and have taken actions. I now believe that whenever I die, my 'Praan' will not try to cling to my body. I also have a practice of saying 'Insha Krishna' (means God Willing), whenever I plan anything for the future. That keeps reminding me that my term could end any time. Yes, I am well prepared to face death.

"Hi Yamaraj. Glad to meet you"

Guilt & Regret: Saint Ramanujar's predecessor, Yamunacharya, while on his death bed, called his disciples, sought pardon if he had hurt their feelings at any time. This is believed to have been done to get rid of any guilt, regret etc. so that Praan can leave body with ease.

Symbolic and Spiritual: Committing to donate all organs is a symbolic way of continuing to 'live' for longer time. Besides, that act could make that person feel good and noble during the last moments.

Celebrating Death: Anthropologist A. M. Hocart, revealed that some primitives in Africa, rejoiced death rather than being afraid of. Incidentally, even today, in Tamil Nadu, some communities celebrate death of those who lived a full life with music and dance during the last journey of the body to the crematorium.

Summary: Death – A promising new beginning

- ✓ ***Conviction in Karma & Reincarnation, which are logical and aligned with the science of evolution of life offer two benefits:***
  - ○ ***Overcoming fear of death.***
  - ○ ***Optimism that death of a body facilitates a new and promising beginning for the soul.***
- ✓ ***Strengthened spirituality reduces desires, attachments, while being prepared lessens worries and anxieties – both support peaceful death.***

JOYFULNESS & HAPPINESS
RECAP/SUMMING UP

"Happiness is the true nature of every human being"

> – *Adi Sankara (700/750, Philosopher, Theologian).*

"Joy is the condition of life"

> – *H D Thoreau (1817/1862, Philosopher, Poet)*

HAPPINESS & JOYFULNESS

Though happiness and joyfulness are used without differentiation, they are different. Listed below are feelings that come under joyfulness *(Adapted from "The Book of Joy" by HH Dalai Lama)*

- Altruism (Happy to make other happy)

- Amusement (Chuckle, Smile)

- Bliss (height of joy)

- Cheerfulness (shows well in facial expressions)

- Contentment (satisfaction)

- Ecstasy (peak happiness)

- Elevation (feeling after an act of compassion)

- Enchantment (delightful contentment)

- Excitement (response to novelty/challenge)

- Exultation (feeling after accomplishment)

- Gratitude (being thankful)

- Happiness (merriment/gaiety)

- Jubilation (feel of delight)

- Laughter (loud, belly laugh)

- Pleasure (comes out of senses)

- Radiant Pride (being joyful when someone close wins an honour)

- Rejoicing (happy for someone else's joy)

- Relief (after overcoming fear, anxiety, stress.)

- Serenity (calmness, peaceful)

- Spiritual radiance (serene joy from well being & benevolence)

- Wonder (feeling of awe, appreciation)

Good News about Happiness

According to several studies, 'seniors are the happiest', substantiated by various studies mentioned below:

> **The U bend factor:** Research held across the world, published in 'The Economist', 2010, reveals that happiness follows the shape of 'U'. People are happy at the beginning of adult life, and then hit a low ('mid life crisis' around 40). And then, as they begin to grow old, they regain happiness which keeps increasing and reaches level of the start of adult life!

> **Increased emotional stability:** In 'Psychology Today, Becky Ready, PhD, shares that compared to youngsters, elders have better emotional stability, which contributes to higher happiness.

> **More positivity:** Article in WebMD, Healthy Ageing, 2017 reports: "When compared to youth, older people are more optimistic, less negative, remember events more positively – all of which contribute to more happiness".

> **Other factors**: A study by Dr. Stranges, University of Warwick, on 10,000 elders in UK and USA, observed that elders are happier due to following:

- Better ability to cope with hardships including pain.

- More comfortable being themselves including being over weight

- Lowered expectations from life, means under lesser pressure.

➤ **Those who are between 65 to 79 are the happiest:** BBC's survey of more than 300, 000 adults in 2016, quoting the Office for National Statistics found that those aged 65 to 79 are the happiest among adults.

➤ **Peaking in skills:** Chris Weller's studies, in the Business Insider Magazine, March 2017, reveal elders can reach peak as follows:

Age	Domains in which Seniors can reach peak
69	Highest life satisfaction (2nd time in one's life)
71	Vocabulary
74	Happiness with one's body
82	Psychological well being

Other reasons why seniors are happiest

- No more Monday morning blues.

- No stress due to unfair organization/boss/rate race.

- No tension about Children's education

- Higher awareness to appreciate & plenty of time to pursue hobbies.

- Very little chance of spouse divorcing

Recap and reinforcement

Following are the A to Z of enhancing happiness

Active: "Tip to live well in old age is to be active and help others" Sarada Menon (98), India's first woman psychiatrist.

Adaptability: Neither wealth nor intelligence, but the ability to adapt is the key to happiness. This has acquired more significance during the Covid pandemic, which further increased stress.

I adapted to the pandemic by spending more time on reading, writing, meditation and listening to music. I also began to enjoy silence and solitude.

Altruism: Quality of deriving happiness from making others happy.

The Reader's Digest (October 2016 & September 2020) mentions following benefits:

- An altruist has a meaning in life and so is happier.

- Joy arising out of doing charitable services lasts longer compared to spending on self or own family.

Anticipation: Anticipating an enjoyable forthcoming event activates pleasure centers in the brain. Sometimes, anticipation is sweeter than the event. That suits seniors more, as they have lot of leisure time

I keep visualizing my time with my granddaughter, months before visiting her, which multiplies my happiness.

Appreciate: The Mother of Aurobindo Ashram narrated the following incident: After the end of First World War, the soldiers returning home were so tired and sick that they were even unable to walk. As they reached their village, the locals came out of their homes, greeted them with song and dance. In a dramatic transformation, the soldiers joined the celebrations, and began to even dance.

Awakening the Child: Acts that do this are - Developing a sense of wonder; Playfulness; Laughter; Curiosity; Creativity; Mischievousness; Being 'Here & Now'.

Over the last decade, I have increased my sense of wonder, and have begun to notice and appreciate not only flowers and clouds but also insects.

Awakening the Child Inside

Art & Craft: The American Art Therapy Association recommends singing, dancing, painting etc. or just appreciating them to experience happiness.

Balance: These comprise following, while the opposites are given in brackets.

- Moderation – Everything in limits (*'swinging to extremes'*)

- Regularity – Consistency. (*'Irregular'*)

- Activity – Action (*'laziness'*).

- Rest – Giving breaks to action (*'restlessness'*)

Baskets of happiness: For many, particularly elders, happiness arises largely from a single source – like caring and spending time with a grandchild. It poses a risk when the child grows up and becomes independent. It's like 'putting all the eggs in one basket'. Instead, it's prudent to diversify and develop joy from many sources including interests and hobbies.

Be yourself: People are happy when they feel free to be themselves. On the contrary, people are unhappy when they try to be like someone else or try hard to make everyone happy.

Once I got a gift, a coffee mug painted with "If you try to please everyone, nobody will like it".

Break from the past: As mentioned earlier, not long ago, the eldest in the family used to decide everything. However, significant changes have taken place. The youngsters like to own responsibility and take decisions. In such cases, elders may break from the past practice of controlling everything, and offer counsel when needed or asked for.

My wife and I gave guidance and the freedom to our son and daughter in choosing their life partners. We are happy because they are happy.

Call without any reason: Drop in or talk to someone (old friend, distant relative, former colleague etc.) without any specific purpose.

I do this regularly. On several occasions, the persons called would not believe me when I say "I just called to say hi", and there is no other reason. Once convinced they became happy.....and relieved too.

Celebrate success of others: Rejoice and share when any person known to you accomplishes anything– it need not be a Bharat Ratna or a Nobel Prize.

When my friend published his first ever e-book, I was the first one to pay, download, post appreciative comment, share the details with all my contacts

Charity begins outside home: Generosity preferably should begin with those who provide services to us and the underprivileged.

For the last 15 years, my wife and I stopped buying new clothes, gifts for ourselves during festivals, birthdays and anniversaries. Instead, we have increased gifting domestic maid, the security guards etc. Also when we performed 'Grihapravesh' of our apartment at Bangalore, we served food to the 250 + construction workers who toiled to build that condominium.

Courtesy begins at home: While many are polite to strangers, but not so with own family members.

Once, a colleague came home for dinner. I appreciated my wife for the food she had prepared. My guest was shocked, and remarked that a husband appreciating his wife is a Western culture, and he had never done that.

Cheerfulness: "If you want to be cheerful, then cheer up someone else" - Mark Twain. Being cheerful is a service to others too. It spreads faster than Covid 19.

Compassion: "If you want others to be happy, practice compassion. If you want yourself to be happy, practice Compassion" said The Dalai Lama.

Harvard Psychologist David McClelland, screened a short film on Mother Teresa's service to poor. He then measured SIgA (indicator of immunity) in the viewers and noticed increase in its levels.

Contentment: Sudha Murty (Chairperson, Infosys foundation) in 'The Old Man and His God', recounts about her meeting a poor, blind old villager who refused monetary help. She summed up the experience:". though I could not agree with his reason (for refusal of help), I noticed he was a contented man, an essential need after a certain age"

De clutter: Many would have accumulated lots of materials, stacked in attics, basements etc., untouched for years. These, in addition to being nuisance, can pose health and fire hazards. Clutter also creates stress. On the contrary, if they are donated while still in good condition, happiness replaces nuisance and hazard.

In my life time, I have moved house about twenty times, and utilised each of this occasion to de-clutter.

Deletions & Additions*: With time, priorities and interests change. It helps to review them periodically to delete those that give tension, and add those which give joy.

I have significantly cut down my time on watching news on TV and reading newspaper since I noticed they generated negativity. Instead, I am utilising that time to listen to classical music, reading, writing and playing outdoor games.

Discover the new you: As mentioned earlier, many are likely to have hidden interests. It is never too late to explore, find at least one and nurture.

Enthusiasm: "Years wrinkle the skin. But lack of enthusiasm wrinkles the soul" said Samuel Ullman (1840/1924, Humanitarian & Poet).

Whenever I am in Chennai I visit a shop that sells rare books, run by an enthusiastic man (85+). Even a small chat with him makes me energized.

Expectations: Keeping them reasonable is the key to avoid disappointments, which is most relevant to elders.

In a Tamizh story 'Yogam' (author late R. Choodamani), the protagonist is a 60 year old mother who continues to help her selfish son even after the latter abandons her. She justifies it with "As a mother, love for my child is instinctive. What matters is that I get joy whenever I care for him. Having understood that, there is no question of me expecting gratefulness from my son and getting disappointed…"

Friends: Maintain old. Make new ones too. Because there's nothing like 'too many friends'.

More and more elders are enjoying reunions with school/college mates, former colleagues than ever before. Another trend is elderly women travelling in groups without their husbands ('less luggage, more comfort'?)

Forgiveness: "Forgive, not because that person deserves, but you need peace. When a person forgives, he does a service to himself"

Many elders tend to carry bitterness for decades, often on trivial matters. The usual advice 'forget and forgive' is difficult since the mind would not easily allow it. An easy solution is given by The Dalai Lama who said "forgetting and forgiving are two different things. While forgetting is difficult, forgiving is easier and that is what needed too".

Gratefulness: Dr. Robert Emmons in The Reader's Digest, 2009, shares findings that those who are grateful, even to small things derive following benefits: More optimism, higher immunity, extra energy and better sleep.

I began to convey my gratefulness before eating food, which I learnt from my granddaughter when she was 3.

Harmony: "When your thought, speech and action are in harmony, that brings happiness"- Mahatma Gandhi.

I have experienced discomfort in me whenever these three are not synchronized.

Helping without expectations: This act offer following benefits as per a house magazine of a hospital: Increases life expectancy, reduces pain, strengthens self confidence, enhances optimism, spreads positivity, creates new relationships and increases happiness.

Hug (after Covid19 threat solution): Benefits of hugging are:

- Improves immunity, memory and wellness
- Reduces pains, hyper tension and fear.
- Strengthens relationships.

From my experience, I would like to add hugging pets and touching tress make me feel good.

Independence: When an elder is able to carry out all the routine tasks by himself, it increases self esteem. Besides, he is also respected more by family members.

Many, including some in late 80's insist on living independently as long as they could manage. If their Children understand the reason, it could help both.

Just Do It: It would do good to go through one's 'Wish List', complete one by one without delaying. Because, for elders, time is ticking.

In a span of about four years after retirement, my wife and I completed visits to more than 150 holy shrines. If we had delayed, our health issues followed by the Pandemic would have made that impossible.

Laugh more: "Laughter is music to your Soul", says an Irish proverb. Laughter offers following benefits: Facial muscles get exercised and relaxed; Respiratory system strengthens; Weight management gets better; Mental health improves; Energy level gets boost; Blood pressure comes down; Pain subsidises; 'Well Being' increases.

Instead of waiting for an occasion to laugh, one can just fake laughter and obtain above benefits since the brain can't differentiate (between real and fake).

I have included forced laughter in my morning yoga.

Learning: "The first step to happiness is a learning mind" says The Dalai Lama. Age should not come in the way to learn anything new, including language, games, music etc. However some hesitate to learn for reasons that include: fear of failure, afraid of ridicule, disillusioned by slow progress etc. All these stumbling blocks can be overcome by changing the outlook to enjoying the learning process.

I took more time than my 10 year old granddaughter to learn the many features of a smart phone. Initially I found it embarrassing but eventually overcame and felt happy that I learnt something new.

Listening: This creates happiness to the person who is listened to as well as who speaks. It also strengthens relationships and increases knowledge.

I have noticed my behaviour of interrupting when someone speaks. I am trying to improve my listening skills - an on-going effort.

Love: In 'Man's Search for Meaning', Viktor Frankl, who was tortured in the concentration camps, shares: "For the first time in my life, I realised the truth and the wisdom - that love is the ultimate goal any man can aspire. Anyone can experience bliss just by contemplation on his beloved ones".

Minimalism: Put simply, it is simple living. Benefits of practicing Minimalism are: freedom from jealousy, stress, worry and fear. It also improves self esteem due to responsible behaviour of not adding to environmental degradation. For example, a cotton T shirt's 'water foot print' is 2925 litres. It means that when you already have enough to wear, and don't get tempted to buy another, you save that much water.

Mood elevators: These include: Sun shine; Breeze; Barefooted walk on sand/grass; looking at sky/water body/flowers & leaves/animal kingdom...the list is endless.

I have begun to do most of the above and vouch for its mood boosting ability.

Move your body: "Even small and frequent body movements, like getting up and walking every ten minutes reduce anxiety" says G Reynolds, in NY Times. Studies also reveal that continued sitting is a more serious health hazard than smoking.

Music: Paul Jenner in 'How to be Happier' lists following benefits of classical music: Increases Oxytocin, the happiness chemical. Lowers cortisol and testosterone (hormones that creates stress and aggression), and increases endorphin (hormone that reduces pain).

Nappiness: Taking short naps (about 20 minutes) in day time improves creativity, strengthens concentration and brings more happiness as per a study in The Daily Mirror, UK.

A 30 minutes nap has been my habit for over 40 years – I managed it even during my work life after convincing my boss that I was meditating on complex issues.

No News = Good News: Some keep worrying about their grand children, spouse or Children, if there is no call or message from them. Instead, if they practice 'No News is Good News', they can relax.

I am doing. My wife is trying.

Nostalgia: *It's* 'a sentimental longing for a period gone by', and is a favourite pastime of many. Research reveals its following benefits: Reduction in feeling of loneliness, boredom and anxiety. Increase in optimism. Improvement in relationships. Enhancement in self-worth. Support in coping with loss.

My family and I enjoy going through old photo albums, and reading letters written on post cards.

Open mindedness: As mentioned earlier, it's a personality trait that helps one to try and enjoy new experiences, which, with conscious effort, can be developed at any age.

In a restaurant, I noticed an elder getting angry when he was served a dish of 'rajma' mixed with ladies finger. He said "these two should never be mixed". However, his wife was relishing it, and was seen enquiring for its recipe.

Optimism: The National Institute of Ageing & The Reader's Digest (Jan. 2017), lists following benefits of being an optimist: Chances of suffering Alzheimer & dementia reduces by 50%.; Stronger heart; Higher immunity; Closer relationships; Sound sleep. Better mental equilibrium.

Pets: Playing with pets reduces hyper tension and relieves stress due to secretion of happiness hormones. However since owning a pet brings huge responsibilities, easier option is to play with someone else's pet or visit a pet day care centre or feed strays.

For the last one year, I am feeding couple of stray dogs. All three of us enjoy.

Play with kids: This is a de-stressor.

The best times of my life have been playing with my granddaughter.

Purpose in life*:* "A meaningful life is the surest path to happiness" observes Dr. Prabha Chandra, Professor of Psychiatrist, NIMHANS, Bengaluru.

Every day as soon as I get up, the first thought that arises is 'What's the enjoyable and meaningful act that's lined up today'. Usually it would be helping someone in need, reading, writing and appreciating the nature.

Pray: 'Scientists find power of prayer', as per 'The Scientific American (2013). Benefits include: Improved self control; increased brain power; higher compassion; faster healing. Interestingly, these benefits increase when one prays for the benefit of someone else.

My wife keeps a list of persons, and prays for them every day.

Responsibility: To be happy, one has to take responsibility for experiencing that. Its corollary is: No one can make you unhappy without your consent.

Read & Share: *"No other activity is as joyful, not sinful, yet everlasting, than the act of reading and sharing" – An Irish Proverb.*

Some recommendations are:

- Make a habit of reading every day (newspaper is not as effective as a book).

- Read variety of genre, authors and languages since studies reveal these increase creativity.

- Sharing excerpts, summary with your family, friends multiply the joy.

I have developed a habit of writing synopsis and review of books and share it with my contacts. I also re-launched a Book Readers' club in our condominium.

Routine – make some, break some: Meaningful routines prevent anxiety, loneliness & depression among seniors ", says Dr.Vijaykumar of NIMHANS, Bengaluru. Examples of routines that do good are related to: food, sleep, medicines, walking etc. Routines that need to be broken to make life spicy are: eating out at a new joint; walk on different routes/ places; getting an Ayurvedic massage etc.

I change directions, routes, timings of my walk. On Sundays, I skip my routines including cycling and yoga.

Self Esteem: It's a feeling of 'self worth'. Anyone, at any age, with efforts can develop and feel it.

A family member (76) was a home maker till she was 65. She then refreshed her skill in playing veena, later learnt to use computer, and for the last eight years, has been conducting on-line classes for students across the world. She shared that this is the happiest phase of her life.

Self – centeredness is a spolier: Larry Scherwitz, Psychologist at University of California, taped conversations of 600 persons, and concluded that those who used the three words - I, Me and Mine – were at the highest risk of heart trouble.

Safe sex: Its benefits to health and happiness have been detailed in an earlier chapter.

Simplify life: "My greatest skill is that my wants are little", said and practiced H D Thoreau, Philosopher (1817/1862).

A few examples applicable to seniors:

- Minimise ownership of fixed assets (e.g. land, house etc)

- If health does not permit, do not undertake responsibility to maintain assets of your Children.

- Reduce number of bank accounts, lockers, vehicles etc.

Social activities: Involving in social activities reduces chances of depression as per study by Gustaf Bostrom, Umea University, Sweden.

My social work after retirement included: Involvement in fund raising and renovation of temple in our ancestral village. After moving to Chennai, my wife and I improved hygiene, housekeeping, air & noise pollution and safety in the neighborhood.

Social Media: These, such as What's App, Telegram, Facebook, Instagram etc. are double edged swords. They can build or destroy relationships.

I reviewed and noticed that on most occasions, they don't enrich my life. I have cut down time spent on them.

Socialise: Tom Rath, Author in 'Life's Great Question...' observes "Socialising is a predictor of human well-being".

The happiness cycle: Being happy stimulates growth of nerve connections, improves cognition (creativity, analytical thinking etc.). These, in turn, create more happiness.

Thoughts: "It is not what you have, or what you are, or where you are that makes you happy, but it is what you think about" said Dale Carnegie (1888/1955. Author, Speaker).

Biological Psychiatry (2011) substantiates: "Your every thought, every emotion has a consequence. Identify and deliberately develop happy thoughts".

Travel: Thomas Gilovich, Psychology Professor, Cornell University said "The level of happiness while buying material things and travel is almost the same. However, while the happiness from a purchase falls over time, whereas from a travel, it remains throughout one's life time"

Volunteering: Any work that suits one's interest and skill can be put into noble use. This action not only raises self esteem, but also diverts attention from negativity.

A woman (75+), in between her treatment for cancer, makes regular visits to a school for deaf and dumb to teach English.

You, First: Remember what a flight attendant says before an aircraft takes off "In the event of low cabin pressure, put your own oxygen mask first, before helping others." The same applies in real life too. Unless one takes care of own happiness, she/he can't make others happy.

Zest for life: Is living each day with a sense of excitement; taking action and change things rather than complaining; looking at the positives, moving forward despite challenges which make life happier and more fulfilling.

I have reviewed the above list.

My happiness score is 78%.

I am taking steps to increase it.

What about you?

Summing Up: With ageing, avenues to derive happiness decline. But, by practicing insights given in this book, new opportunities can be found to increase happiness. I am doing. You too can.

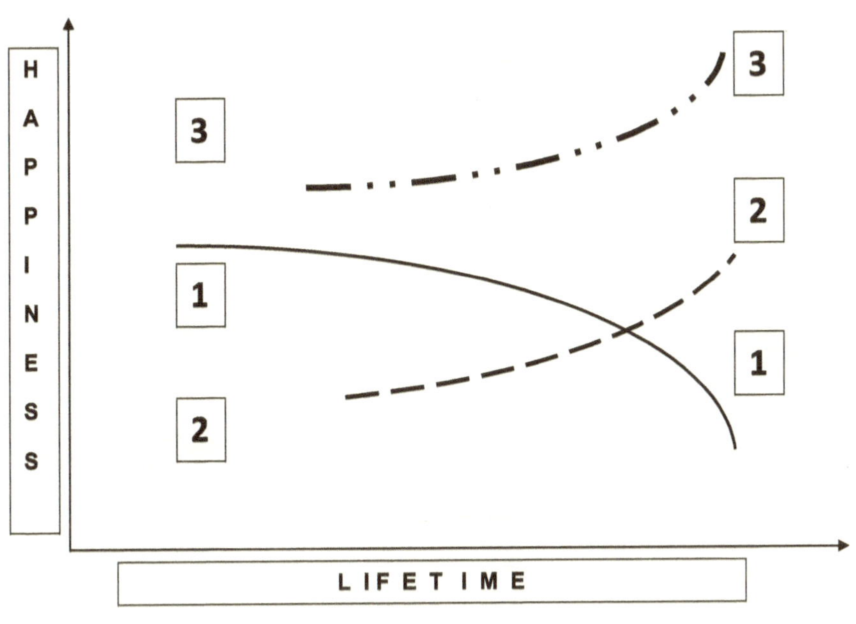

CURVE No.	CURVE DESCRIPTION
1	Decreasing opportunities to derive happiness due to ageing
2	Increasing happiness by following insights given in this book
3	Net Result - Increasing Happiness with age.

And the senior lived more happily than ever before

Not The End...
But a Beginning
For
Increased Happiness

www.ingramcontent.com/pod-product-compliance
Lightning Source LLC
Chambersburg PA
CBHW031549150726

47990CB00001B/271